ALL ABOUT
Modelling Australian Animals
Professional Series

CREATED AND WRITTEN BY
MICHAEL GODDARD

PHOTOGRAPHY BY MICHAEL GODDARD

BAKE TRAIN

Disclaimer

I wish to state that no animals were hurt nor abused in the making of this book.

To the memory of George Stevens

George started his career as a young lad at the high class confectioners Patterson and Hughes in Birmingham England and finished it by teaching the chefs of Queen Elizabeth II.
His skills with marzipan were second to none and he actually did a number of pieces for E. Storer's "The Complete Book of Marzipan".

Many of the chef lecturers at The Birmingham College of Food who won medals at Hotel Olympia in the 1980s had him to thank for the skills he passed on. I was lucky enough to be able to sit in on their sessions as a bakery student and saw most of the centre pieces they worked on.
George Stevens' love of marzipan modelling and cake decoration was the greatest inspiration I'll ever have.

About this book

The crazy world of Australian animals, whether they originate from here or were brought here, we certainly have our fair share of unique creatures.

Who would have thought that a British scientist would stick a duck's bill to a cat's body and then add webbed feet, add a strange looking tail and make up some cock and bull story about it laying eggs just to make a name for himself? But of course this didn't happen it was our duck billed platypus that, although so unbelievable, is actually a much revered animal here in Australia.

In this book I have tried to epitomise the animals we have in our own back yard while giving them a character that makes them a talking piece when used as a decoration on your cakes or in a centre piece.

Foreword

I first met Mike when he attended my Cake Decorating Class in Hobart, to further his skills in the area of Sugar Flowers. With his training in the U.K. and Switzerland in Cake Decorating and Patisserie, he proved to be a very apt student, excelling in Royal Icing, Chocolate and Marzipan Modelling.

Mike is a member of the Hobart Branch of the Cake Decorators Association of Tasmania and has willingly shared his vast knowledge with us. At the Australian National Seminar, held in Launceston in 2011, hosted by Tasmania, he was the guest demonstrator for our State. It was there, that he first introduced the delegates to some of the Australian animals featured in this book.

Mike is a humble man, very creative and has a great sense of humour which is illustrated in his marzipan work.

This book will delight children purely as a story book with the text and expertly moulded characters. I am also sure Cake Decorators throughout the world will find a special place on their bookshelves for "All About Modelling Australian Animals".

Congratulations Mike, I am honoured to be asked to write this foreword.

Betty Debnam

Contents

Disclaimer	2
To the memory of George Stevens	2
About this book	2
Hygiene	6
Moulds	6
Yeasts	6
Various Marzipans	7
Cake Marzipan	7
Modelling Marzipan	7
Raw Marzipan	7
Made Modelling Pastes	7
Marzipan Modelling Pastes	8
Recipe A	8
Recipe B	8
Recipe C	9
Plastic Icing/Rolled Fondant/RTR	10
Dusting Materials	10
Colouring	10
Permitted Colours	10
Types of Colours	10
Royal Icing	11
Fresh Egg White / Albumen	11
Dried Egg White / Albumen	11
Actiwhite and Albumen Substitutes	11
Albumen to water proportions	11
Sugar	11
Sugar to Egg White proportions	12
Glycerine/Glycerol	12
Acids	12
Whiteness	12
Making Royal Icing	13
Making royal icing by machine	13
Problems with royal icing	14
Piping Chocolate for eyes	14
Products	15
Varnishes	15
Cocoa butter	15
Powdered Gum Arabic	15
Glue	15

Equipment	16
Let's Model	18
Weighing or portioning marzipan	18
Basic shapes	19
Camel	20
Crocodile	24
Echidna	30
Fairy Penguins	34
Koalas	38
Kookaburras	42
Octopus	46
Parrot	50
Platypus	54
Possum	58
Roo and little Joey	62
Seagulls	66
Sheep	70
Soldier Crabs	72
Tassie Devil	76
Tree Frog	80
Turtles	84
Wabbits	88
Wombat	92
Rock Sugar	96
Isomalt	98
About the Author	99

Hygiene

Marzipan is susceptible to moulds and yeasts.

Moulds

Moulds will grow on marzipan if excess moisture is present as the nuts used to make the marzipan contain protein that is necessary for mould growth. Moulds don't just grow on the surface, they send roots deep into the product they are living on. These roots deposit toxins (alpha toxins) deep into the food they grow on. These toxins can have a long term detrimental effect on the liver.

Yeasts

Wild yeasts, present in the atmosphere, can get mixed into the marzipan during moulding which later start fermentation. These yeasts act on the sugar content of the marzipan (yeast requires moisture, food and warmth to work – all present with marzipan). Fermentation is also caused through secondary fermentation caused by enzymes in flour dust present in the bakery or by food colours due to poor hygiene practices. Osmophylic yeasts present on your hands also get mixed into the marzipan and can cause the marzipan to ferment too if the temperature is suitable for it to happen.

The most important aspect of using marzipan is hygiene as someone is going to eat what you have just modelled with your hands. Your work surface, utensils and hands must be sanitised to ensure total hygiene. Tables and equipment can be washed down and sanitised with a sanitiser.

Note

Sanitisers need time to work and should be left on the surface of the table – wiping with a "clean" dish cloth can re-introduce bacteria from the cloth onto the table.

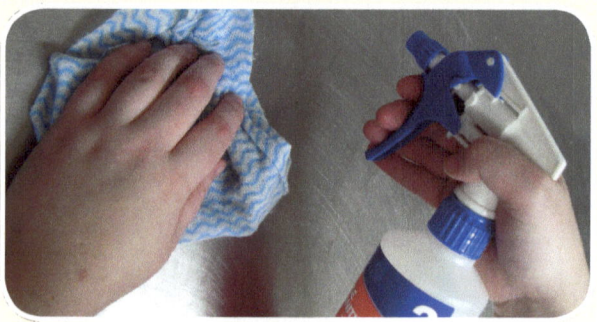

Wash and dry your hands thoroughly for hygiene purposes. This also needs to be done at regular intervals during modelling as the moisture on your hands attracts the sugar in the marzipan and after a while a build-up occurs which creates a sticky surface preventing the models from having a smooth surface.

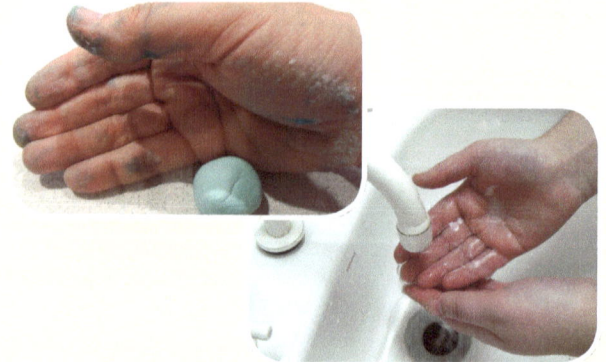

Various Marzipans

Various Marzipans can be purchased in three (3) forms **Cake Marzipan, Modelling Marzipan** and **Raw Marzipan.**

Cake Marzipan

Is a ready to use product containing one third (1/3) almonds and two thirds (2/3) sugar. It can be used straight from the packet and can be purchased in neutral or yellow (a tradition dating back to when egg was used to bind the marzipan).

Modelling Marzipan

Is a paste much smoother than cake marzipan so that fine definition may be obtained when modelling. It contains a higher proportion of almonds that are finely ground. The proportions are approximately 1:1 sugar to almonds although more glucose and sugar can be added to make the models more cost effective effective. *See recipes for modelling paste.*

Raw Marzipan

Is an ingredient used to produce other items. It contains two thirds (2/3) almonds and one third (1/3) sugar. It cannot be used straight from the packet for modelling or coating cakes as the high oil content would cause it to oil quickly leading to a crumbly marzipan that will also stain any icing it may come in contact with. This too is neutral in colour but is darker in colour as well as this it has a more pronounced almond flavour. To make this paste into a modelling or coating paste the modeler can add warm glucose, icing sugar and in some cases invert sugar which prevents oiling when working with it. Raw marzipan can also be used as a substitute for ground almonds in baked products.

Made Modelling Pastes

Although cake marzipan can be used for modelling it is better that a purchased paste such as the one above is used or one is made from raw marzipan. This will produce a paste with better handling qualities due to its consistency.

On the next page are recipes with varying keeping qualities.

Marzipan Modelling Pastes

Recipe A

Models made from this recipe can be kept for up to three months

INGREDIENT	METRIC	IMP	%	METHOD
Raw Marzipan	2.720	6lbs 0oz	100	Heat the glucose and invert sugar to +/- 80°C (180°F).
Icing Sugar	2.040	4lbs 0oz	75	Add to the marzipan and mix to a smooth paste in a machine bowl using a dough hook on 1st speed. Blend in the icing sugar.
Glucose	0.200	7oz	7.3	
Invert Sugar *	0.200	7oz	7.3	Keep in an airtight container or plastic bags to prevent drying out and crusting.

* A syrup of glucose (dextrose) and leavulose (fructose) produced by boiling sucrose with a weak acid. Invert sugar will not crystallize.

Recipe B

Models made from this recipe do not keep as well as those made from the paste above.

INGREDIENT	METRIC	IMP	%	METHOD
Raw Marzipan	2.720	6lbs 0oz	100	Heat the glucose to +/- 80°C (180°F).
Icing Sugar	2.040	4lbs 0oz	75	Add to the marzipan and mix to a smooth paste in a machine bowl using a dough hook on 1st speed. Blend in the icing sugar.
Glucose	0.510	1lb 7oz	18.8	Keep in an airtight container or plastic bags to prevent drying out and crusting.

The glucose must be heated to prevent the marzipan oiling. The icing sugar can be reduced by up to 50% and replaced with caster sugar to give the marzipan a 'bite'.

Models made from this recipe can remain soft for up to 3 months.

Recipe C

This recipe is the same as "A" but is made using marzipan with 50:50 (1 part almond to 1 part sugar.)

INGREDIENT	METRIC	IMP	%	METHOD
50:50 Marzipan	1.000	6lbs 0oz	**100**	Heat the glucose and invert sugar to +/- 80°C (180°F). Add to the marzipan and mix to a smooth paste in a machine bowl using a dough hook on 1st speed. Blend in the icing sugar. Keep in an airtight container or plastic bags to prevent drying out and crusting.
Icing Sugar	0.400	4lbs 0oz	**40**	
Glucose	0.075	7oz	**7.3**	
Invert Sugar *	0.075	7oz	**7.3**	

Plastic Icing/ Rolled Fondant/ RTR

Due to the cost of marzipan and the fact that there are a lot of people who do not like the mouth feel or flavour of marzipan it can be substituted for plastic icing (RTR/rolled fondant). It may be necessary to "tighten" it up with some CMC (Tylose or Cekol) powder so that the weight of the pieces doesn't compact the lower shapes.

Dusting Materials

When working with marzipan only dust the work surface and top off the marzipan with pure icing sugar as cornflour (wheaten) contains enzymes that will start fermentation. When dusting the top of the marzipan with icing sugar it should be rubbed in to prevent white patches appearing on the finished surface. To finely dust marzipan a small bag made from muslin cloth can be filled with icing sugar or pure cornflour/corn starch which is gently shaken over the marzipan or table.

Colouring

Permitted Colours

Use only 'permitted' food colours to colour marzipan. Colour application can be achieve by any of the following methods

1. **Mixing in** by hand for small quantities and by machine for larger quantities
2. **Painting** using a paint brush.
3. **Spraying** with an artist's airbrush. Use a 5% concentration of food dye in water and mix one third of this with two thirds pure alcohol – this dries quicker and allows you to get more depth in your colour.
4. **Spraying** with proprietary food spray cans such as gold or silver.
5. **Singeing** using a blow torch.

Types of Colours

1. **Liquids** use for normal production.
2. **Powders** used where deeper colours are required should be reconstituted as a concentrate.
3. **Pastes** used where deeper colours are required.

Adding more and more liquid colour to achieve a deeper colour will result in a softer paste that will become sticky, difficult to mould and will not retain its shape.

Royal Icing

This is basically a meringue as it is also made of eggwhites and sugar but in this case the sugar is icing sugar and the proportion of sugar is much higher than a normal meringue.

Fresh Egg whites/Albumen

Fresh egg whites tend to be gelatinous and have a slight yellow tinge which is imparted to the icing. The resultant icing can sometimes be "pudding like" in consistency. Fresh whites beat up better if allowed to stand a few hours before use as their acidity changes (pH). If stood over night some of their water content evaporates off and they will then beat up better as the protein content present will be stronger.

Dried Egg whites/Albumen

This can be purchased as a powder or in crystal form and are dried forms of the above. These also give a slight yellow tinge to the icing but the icing is less pudding like as the albumen is denatured during the drying process. Some of these need to be soaked for 24 hours and will need to be stirred occasionally. It is advisable to strain them prior to use to remove any undissolved bits.

Actiwhite and Albumen Substitutes

These have no colour and are not gelatinous. They produce good smooth icings and are now used extensively in bakeries and patisseries as they require little or no soaking prior to use.

NOTE: Actiwhite is a trade name belonging to Bakels.

Albumen to water proportions

INGREDIENT	IMPERIAL	IMPERIAL OUNCES	RATIO	METRIC g
Water	1 pt	20	10	1000
Albumen/Substitute	3 oz	3	1.5	150

Sugar

The sugar should be sieved through a very fine sieve to ensure it is free of lumps and large crystals which will block the fine writing tubes/nozzles/pipes.

There are two types of icing sugar used in Australia:- pure and icing mixture.

Icing mixture is not suitable for making royal icing as it is a mixture of icing sugar and starch which prevents lumping. The starch breaks down the egg white structure during mixing and is unable to take in air resulting in a mix that does not retain its shape properly when piped.

Pure icing sugar contains no starch and therefore has no adverse effect on the icing.

Identification of icing sugar can be made in one of two ways:

1. When mixed into water pure icing sugar goes clear and icing mixture goes cloudy.

2. Mix a small amount of the suspect icing sugar with some water and add a drop or two of iodine. If starch is present the mix will go purple/black. If no starch is present no colour change will be observed.

Sugar to eggwhite proportions

INGREDIENT	IMPERIAL	IMPERIAL OUNCES	RATIO	METRIC g
Icing Sugar	7 lbs	112	5.6	5600
Albumen/Substitute	1 pt	20	1	1000
Glycerine	½ - 1 oz	½ - 1	0.3 - 0.8	16 - 45

Glycerine/Glycerol

This is a substance classified as a humectant and is capable of attracting and giving off moisture when in the appropriate atmospheric condition.

Glycerine doesn't keep icing soft but allows it to set hard without it being brittle. When stacking or tiering wedding cakes it allows the cake to be tiered without the aid of wooden skewers through the cake and also allows the icing to be cut easily.

However, if too much glycerine is added the dried icing has a tendency to be powdery and is easily damaged if knocked. Glycerine should be added towards the end of mixing as once it is added the icing takes in air more rapidly making it difficult to coat with.

Acids

These strengthen the protein in the albumen and results in a hard flinty icing making it difficult to cut. Acids should be added when producing run-outs (flood in work) or when doing extension work or suspended line work.

Acid varieties

Citric (lemon juice)
Tartaric (dissolve crystals in water)
Cream of Tartar
Acetic (vinegar)

Whiteness

Blue colour can be added to royal icing to improve the whiteness (as is done with washing powders). The blue reflects the light more and makes the icing whiter.

DO NOT ADD blue colour if other delicate colours are to be added as their true colour will be distorted by the blue.

Blue colour should always be diluted before adding to the royal icing. This can be done in one of two ways:

1. Dilute a measured amount of blue colour with a set amount of water.

2. Mix some blue colour into an amount of royal icing and then add a small amount of this blue icing to the bulk of the icing.

Making royal icing

Royal icing is a type of heavy meringue which is a beaten up foam consisting of a protein structure that carries the sugar.

Royal icing should be stiff enough, when made, to stand in peaks and keep its shape. This can only be achieved by practice. The stiffness of the icing can be achieved in one of two ways

1. Air (as with meringue the mix stiffens as air is beaten into it).
2. Icing sugar (the mix becomes doughy as more sugar is beaten in).

A good royal icing is a perfect blend of icing sugar, albumen and air.

If too much air is beaten in the mix will resemble a meringue and will be too airy to obtain a smooth coating consistency. However, if too much sugar is added then the mix becomes stodgy, will not spread or pipe easily and will not dry properly because the mix needs to be slightly porous to dry (like a cake needs to be aerated to make the passage of heat to its centre easily). The beating in of the air acts as an oxidising agent and whitens the icing.

If the icing is not stiff enough with the correct combination of air and sugar it will appear glossy and will not be white, it will not dry and it will be impossible to tier wedding cakes in the traditional manner as the pillars will have a tendency to sink into the cake.

When the correct consistency is achieved the glycerine and blue colour can be added. A good practice is to "meter" the colour in so as to obtain the same colour every time.

Making royal icing by machine

Wash the machine bowl and beater thoroughly in hot water to remove any grease. Place the reconstituted albumen in the machine bowl (DO NOT USE tin plated bowls as they will rust and discolour the icing) also plastic bowls tend to harbour grease. Add the required amount of sieved icing sugar and stir in, to wet the sugar. Using the beater, mix on slow speed until the required consistency is achieved, adding more sugar if required.

When mixed keep the icing covered with a clean, damp tea towel to prevent the mix crusting.

When standing in the bowl the mix will tend to break down and will then have a coarse texture, this can be made smooth again by mixing on the machine again or by stirring with a spoon.

Problems with royal icing

As with meringue every attempt should be made to keep fat away from the eggwhites as it will shorten the protein and will not allow to foam properly resulting in an icing which lacks stiffness and can be sloppy in nature

Coarse texture is due to the icing having been stood for a period of time and has started to break down.

A light and fluffy icing is due to over beating, this can be stood for a period of time and then stirred to break down the coarse bubbles.

Lumps in the icing are due to not sieving the sugar or using too coarse a sieve which allows large crystals of sugar through, these large crystals block up the fine piping tube used for line work and writing.

Piping chocolate for eyes

Scaling Weight: 600gms		Yield: 600gms	

STAGES	INGREDIENTS	WEIGHT	%
	Shortening	125	*71.4*
	Cocoa Powder	175	*100*
*	Syrup	300	*171*
	Totals	600	*342.4*

STAGES	INGREDIENTS	WEIGHT	%
Syrup	Water	250	*100*
	Castor Sugar	250	*100*
	Glucose	125	*50*
	Totals	625	*250*

Method:

Boil the ingredients for the syrup together and cool to 70-80°C.

Melt the shortening and cool to 50 – 60°C.

Stir the cocoa powder into the shortening in two additions with a whisk.

Strain the syrup and stir into the chocolate mix.

Pour into a plastic container then scrape down and cover with a cloth until cold, place a lid on top and store in the fridge until required.

Reheat in a microwave in small amounts in a small container until warm and fluid.

Products

Varnishes

Known as confectioner's varnish, marzipan lacquer is the varnish applied to marzipan, gum paste and chocolate to preserve the item's gloss, prevent it drying out too quickly and to give it better eye appeal.

A non–edible varnish can be produced by dissolving gum benzoin in rectified spirits of wine but this must only be used for non-edible decorative display work. Marzipan is usually varnished with a solution of white shellac in Isopropyl alcohol as it is a high proof alcohol and evaporates quickly leaving a thin layer of the shellac on the product. If making this type of varnish do not use normal shellac as it is poisonous and do not use polyurethane varnish.

Food grade varnishes can also be purchased in aerosol cans.

Cocoa Butter

Cocoa butter can also be bought in an aerosol can and used as a varnish.

Powdered Gum Arabic

Powdered Gum Arabic can be mixed with water (10ml of Gum Arabic to 60ml of water) to produce an edible varnish for marzipan and rolled fondant. When used as a varnish several layers may be required to obtain a high gloss.

Glue

Use the gum Arabic solution listed in varnishes. This can be painted on when used as a glue to join modelled pieces together.

Make a solution using Tylopur / tylose / colegan. This can be kept in an air tight container for months and is what most cake decorators use in Australia.

Equipment

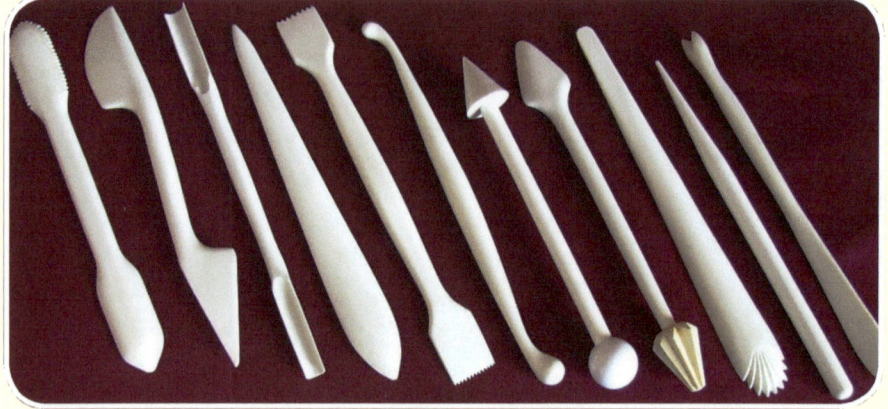

Modelling Tools

Various textured rolling pins

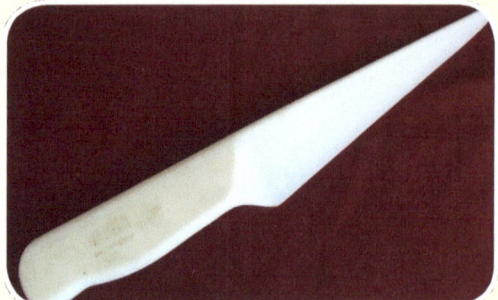

Marzipan Knife

Tooth brush for speckling

Textured Plate

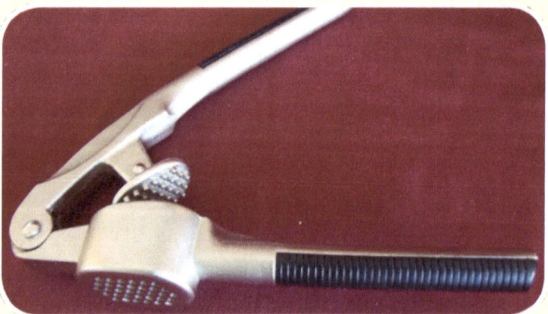

Garlic press for making hair and grass

Clear Perspex for rolling cylinder shapes

Pastry/cookie cutters

Air brush and compressor

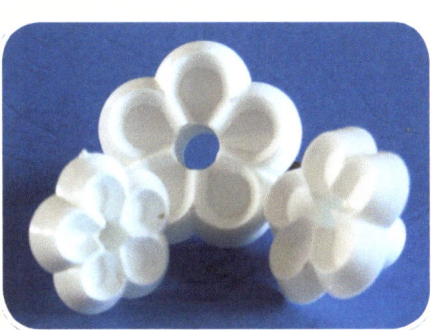

Blossom cutters

17

Let's Model

The approximate amount of marzipan required for the job in hand should be sliced off not pulled off with the fingers (this makes for a bigger surface area that has to be cut off if it dries hard resulting in more wastage than if it were sliced straight). The remainder should be wrapped or stored in an airtight container with any excess paste not required being returned to the airtight container. If it crusts warm it gently in a microwave and rub it down on the table, this also applies to rolled fondant.

Weighing or portioning marzipan

If making a number of models all the same our production can be rationalised by dividing the modelling medium into the appropriate weights for the models and can be achieved in a number of ways

- Scaling where each piece is weighed individually, this can be time consuming and tedious.

- Taking a set amount to produce a specific number of pieces rolling this out to a cylindrical shape and a certain length and then cutting it e.g. 100g rolled out to 10 cm and cut every 2 cm would produce 5 pieces at 20g.

- Roll out the marzipan to a set thickness and cut out with specific sized pastry cutters. 55mm thick cut with 50mm Ø cutter will provide a 32g weight.

Having taken sufficient paste it has to be coloured and worked until it is smooth and until there are no visible seams on the surface. Now it can be shaped.

Basic Shapes

1. Ball
2. Pear
3. Cylinder
4. Cone
5. Tear drop

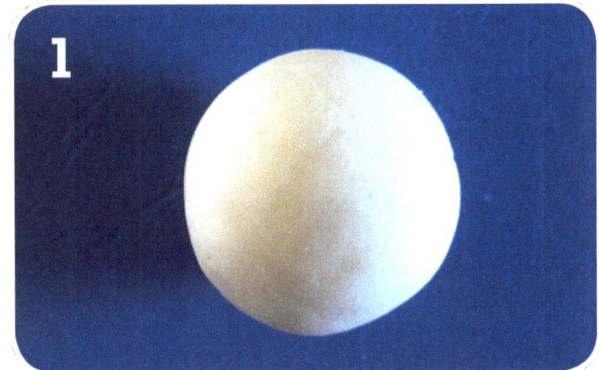

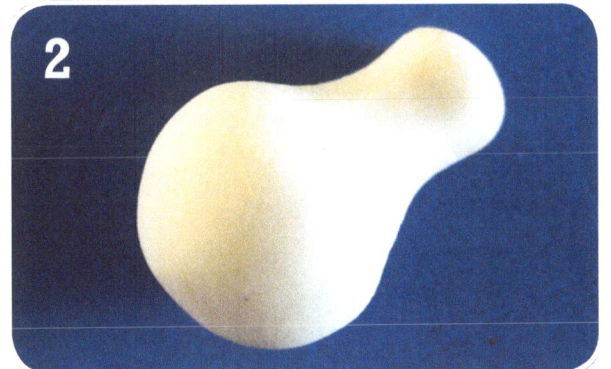

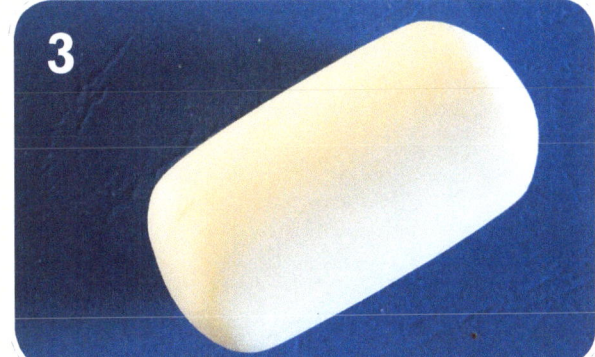

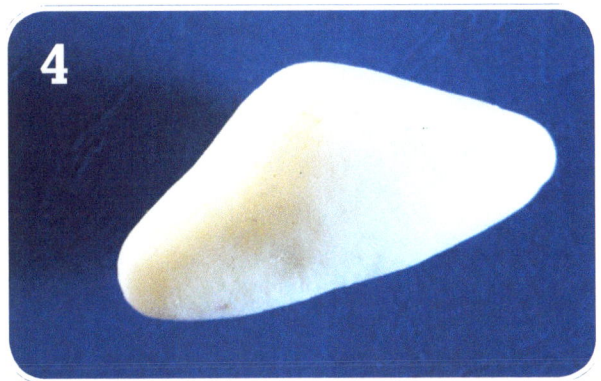

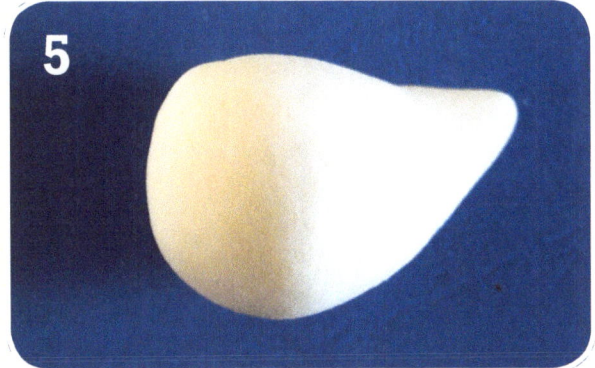

Carmel the Camel

Carmel loves to trek across the desert to see the Western Australian wild flowers in spring time.

It's time to fill up, no good going on a long trip in the Outback without sufficient fuel.

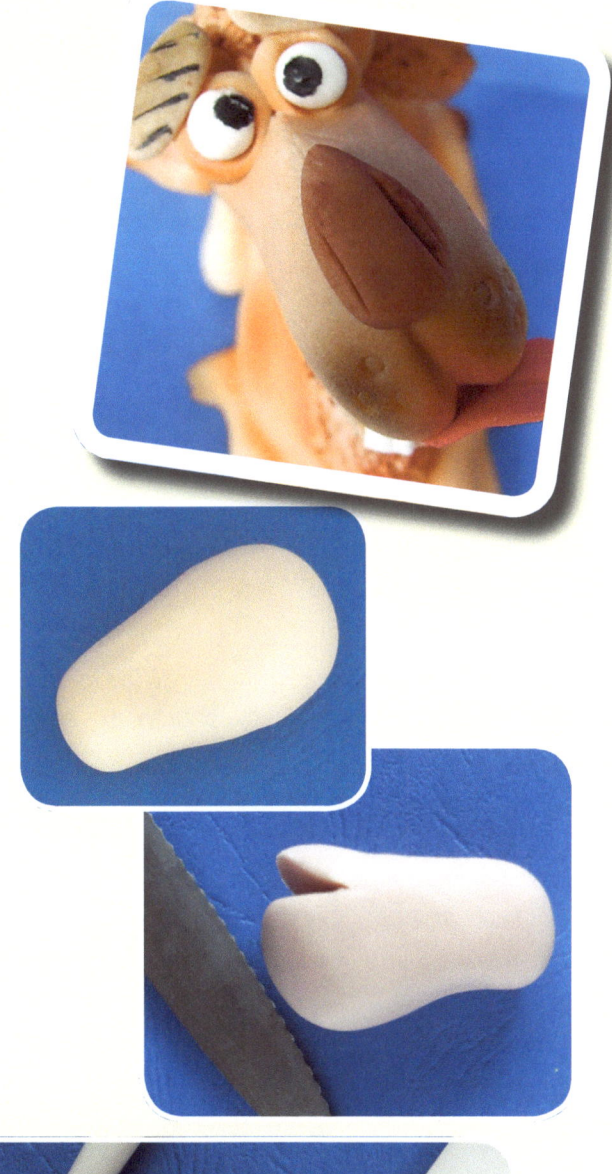

PART	WEIGHT	COLOUR
Body and neck	70g	Cream
Head	20g	Cream
Legs and toes	10g x 4	Cream
Tail	2g	Brown
Hair		Brown
Wall		Cream
Bowser base		Blue
Bowser	70g	Blue
Bowser gauge	12g	Blue
Bowser gauge face		White
Signs	15g	White
Hose	10g	White
Nozzle	2g	Grey
Filter	2g	White

Head

Shape the head as a dumpy dumbbell.

Cut the mouth with a knife.

Shape the lower jaw with the bone tool.

Make a groove above the mouth.

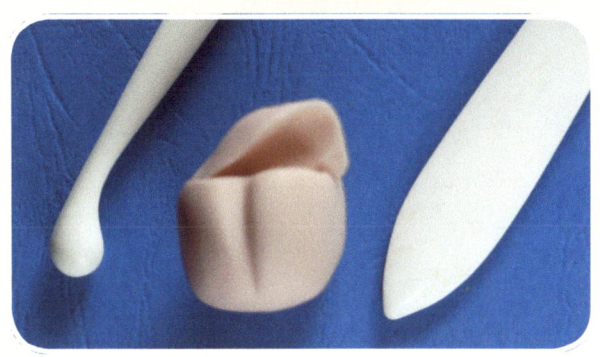

Pinch the top to make a ridge.

Widen the groove just above the mouth with the bone tool.

Attach the nose and make two nostril grooves.

Add two small balls for eye sockets and press into position with the bone tool. Stick with Tylose.

Attach two tear drops for ears using Tylose and press into place with the bone tool.

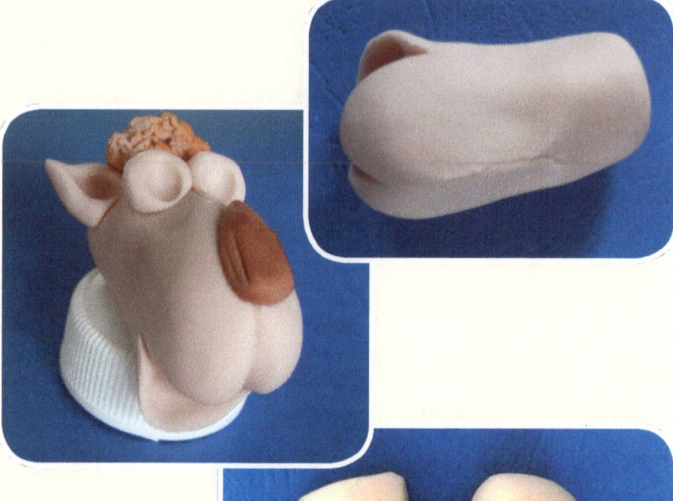

Body
Form the body as in the photograph.

Thin out the edge of the mound on the left to for the neck.

Set aside to firm up.

Legs and feet
Make the legs and feet as in the photograph, approx. 75mm long.

Attach the legs bending them as in the photograph.

Hair
Make the hair by pushing some modelling paste through a sieve, make sure it is moist otherwise it falls to bits later.

Attach the hair to the hump, the head and the neck.

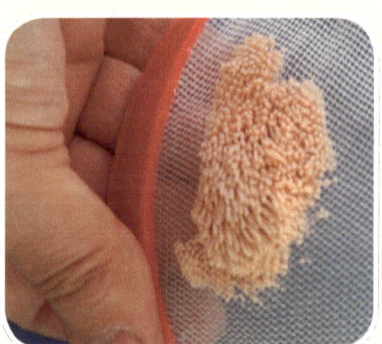
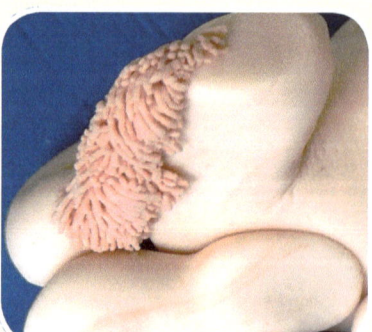
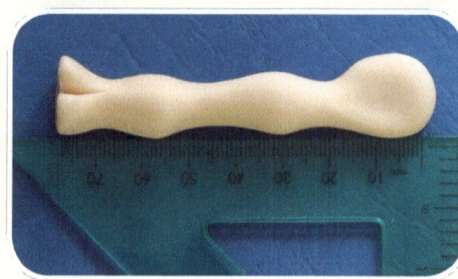
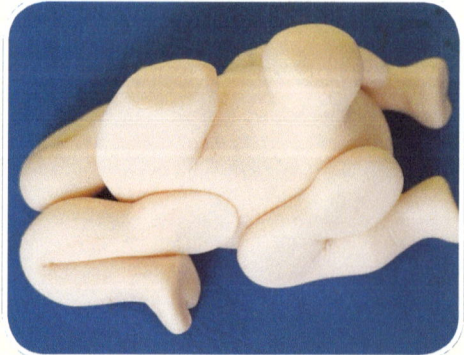

Spray
Spray all the parts.

Brick wall
Make a sheet of modelling paste +/- 4mm thick mark with a brick pattern and set aside to dry on Styrofoam. Spray and add the signage.

Water pump
Make the parts for water pump, set side to dry.

Spray parts in a deeper blue.

Assemble the water pump as in the photograph.

Finishing Touches
Give the camel some teeth and a tongue. Add the whites of the eyes and paint on the pupils or pipe in dark chocolate.

Add the wall, water pump, sign post notice board, and some sand (use polenta).

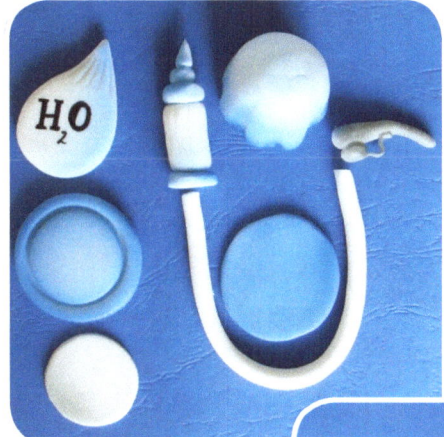
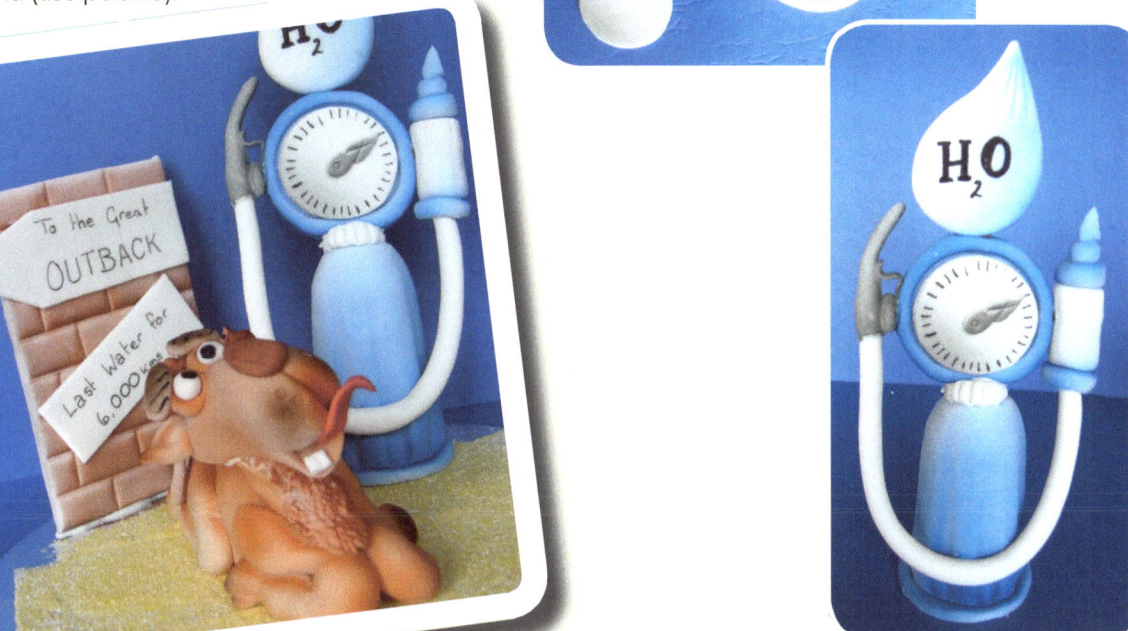

Crocodile
...sad because no one wants to play

Crocodiles are such delicate creatures that have very few friends to play with – 'cos they eat them – and then get sad because no one wants to play. Then come the crocodile tears 'till their mummies console them – or they drown!

PART	WEIGHT	COLOUR
Tail	55g	Green
Body	50g	Green
Head	30g	Green
Eye sockets	1g ÷ 2	Green
Legs	5g x 2	Green
Arms and hands	5g x 2	Green
Nostrils	1g ÷ 2	Green

Tail

Shape the tail as a long thin taper and mark with a curved tool then crimp down each side with curved pastry crimpers.

Turn the tail over and mark rectangles on the other side.

Shaping the tail

Drape the tail and curve it over a small bowl and allow it to set in that position.

Body
Make an egg shape.

Pin out a pale brown piece of paste and attach it to the front of the body.

Mark the front with squares and crimp down the sides with curved crimpers.

Mark the back of the body with a row of curved marks and crimp either side.

Legs and feet
Make the legs and mark them with squares with a modeling tool.

Head
After moulding the paste round form it into a pear shape.

Form the mouth
Next use a pair of scissors to cut the mouth at the narrow end.

Now use a dog bone tool to shape the mouth open.

Markings for the head
Mark rectangles on the head.

Nostrils
Attach two balls for nostrils using Tylose and press them into place with a dog bone tool.

Eye sockets
Attach larger balls in the same manner as the nostrils.

Eyes
Make two small balls of paste and place into the eye sockets. Use the curved tool to mark the eye balls so that they look as if the model is squinting.

Shaping the mouth
Open the mouth and place a small piece of dowel (6mmØ) across it to keep it open while it dries.

Assembly
When the tail is dry attach the body to it with Tylose then attach the legs.

Spray
Spray the front of the body reddish brown then spray the rest of the model brown. Spray a little deeper around the edge of the mouth and the nostrils and eye sockets.

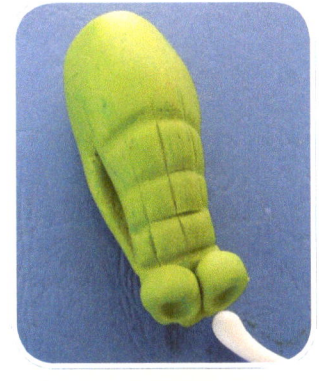
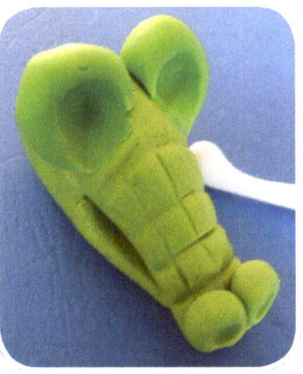

Teeth and tongue

Make the tongue by shaping a tear drop and making a crease down its centre. Next spray it pink and set aside to dry. When dry place into the mouth.

Make the teeth as small tear drops and attach to the top and bottom jaws.

Pool of tears

Follow the instructions at the rear of the book for cooking isomalt and pour out onto a Silpat or Teflon mat. Allow to cool completely.

Tears

Be sure to wear gloves when doing this next operation!

Very carefully half fill a silicone paper piping bag with liquid isomalt. Seal the bag well. Cut off a small tip from the end pipe comma shapes onto a Silpat mat or Teflon sheet. Set aside to cool and set.

Arms

Shape the arms as in the picture making sure you make a left and right arm.

Mark with the curved ended tool.

Hanky

Roll out a thin piece of paste, cut it into a square and pinch in the centre. Spray the ends if required.

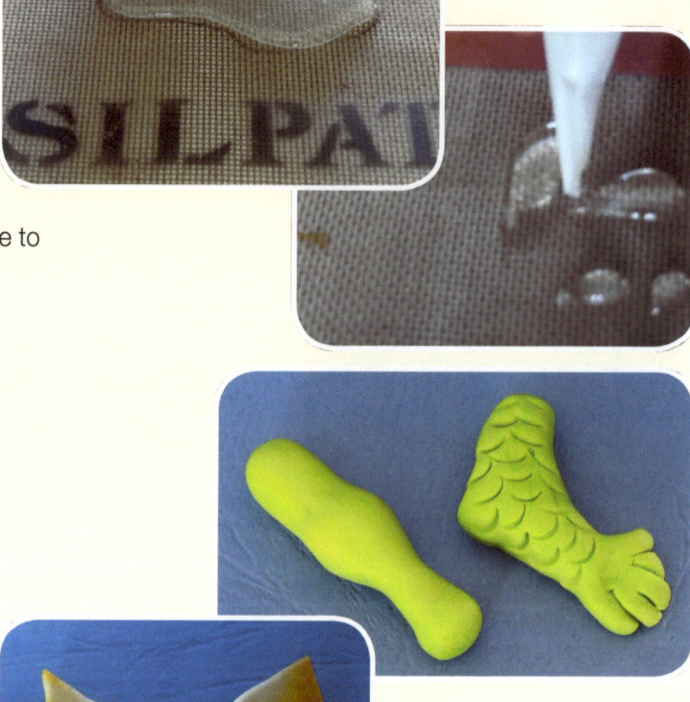

Next

Position the pool of tears in place.

Sit the body onto the pool.

Attach the head to the body.

Finishing Touches

Attach the arms with Tylose and spray to match the body.

Position the hanky.

Attach the tears by making small holes in the corners of the eyes and placing the pointed ends of the tears in the holes.

Attach some tears to the pool.

Other accessories include some stones and grass.

Echidna

...*a great day to be lazy and sun-bake.*

It's a great day to be lazy and sun-bake. Lunch always shows up just when it's time to eat. Mmm they're so small but I just love them when they come coated in chocolate!

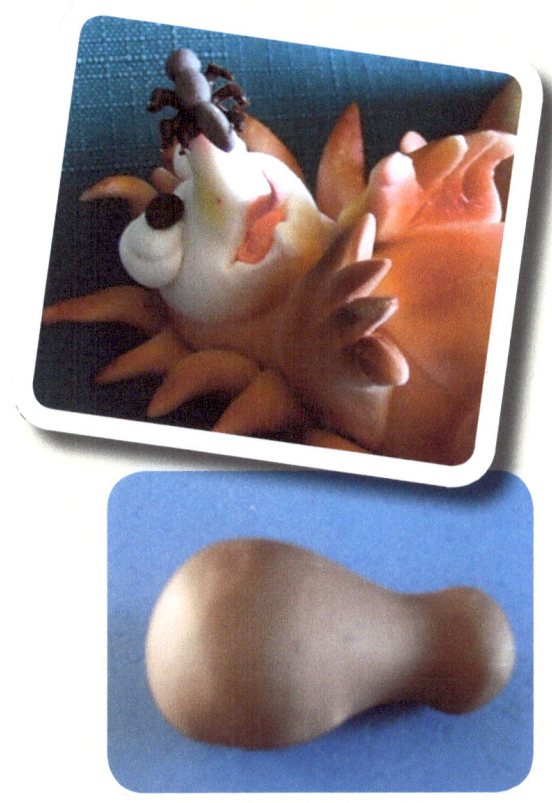

PART	WEIGHT	COLOUR
Body	45g	Dark brown
Face	8g	White
Tongue	1g	Pink
Spikes	Various	Coffee brown
Feet	3g x 4	Brown
Tummy	7g	White
Eyes	1g ÷ 2	White

Body and head
Form a pear shape with brown icing for the body.

Make an indent in the top and bottom.

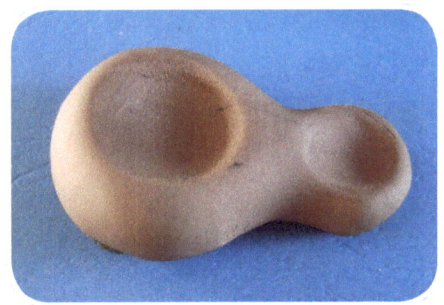

Muzzle
Produce a tear drop for the muzzle.

Next cut the mouth with a pair of scissors.

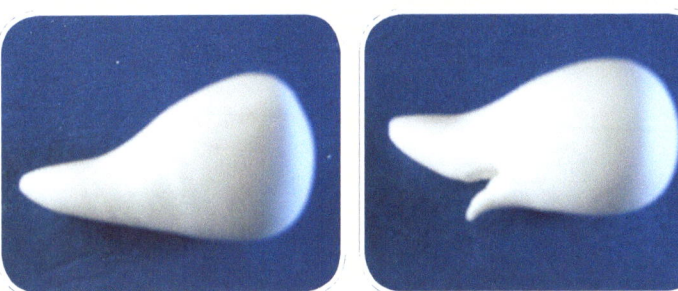

31

Attaching muzzle, eye sockets and tummy

Place the muzzle in place using Tylose.

Make a ball of white icing and place that in the larger indent for the tummy.

Make two small balls for the eye sockets and press into place on the top part of the muzzle.

The model will now look like this.

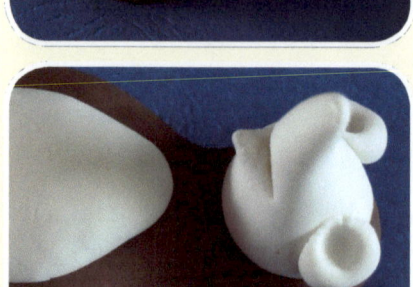

Spines

Make some small carrot shapes.

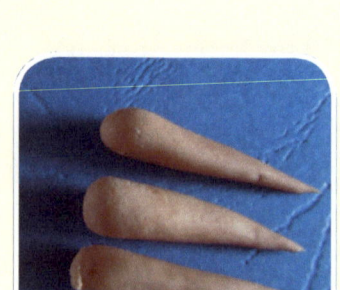

Attaching the spines

Use Tylose. Attach these as a first layer around the model keeping them fairly upright.

This is what it should look like.

Second row of spines

Attach a second layer of spines below the first.

Feet

Make the echidna's feet from balls that are pressed down to form a wedge shape.

Cut three triangles out of the tapered edge.

Finishing Touches

Finally attach a curled tongue and pipe in the eyes using royal icing and chocolate.

Here an ant has been made by making the body from modelling paste and by piping chocolate legs onto paper after which the body is placed on top.

Accessories

The ant hill is made from a cone of modelling paste covered with semolina.

The grass was pressed through a garlic press.

Fairy Penguins
They dance around their sand castles…

These little fellas only come out to play as the sun goes down and the stars come out.

They dance around their sand castles and bewitch everyone that sees them. Their fairy wings can't be seen by humans but my special camera caught the sight just for you.

PART	WEIGHT	COLOUR
Body and head	70g	White
Feet	2 x 1g	Pink
Fairy wings	2 x 1g	Pink
Penguin wings	2 x 1g	Pink
Beak	1g	Peach
Eyebrows	1g	White

Body and head
Shape the body as a dumbbell using white modelling paste with one end larger than the other.

For the reclining penguin bring the larger end to a point.

For a standing penguin make the end flat for it to stand on.

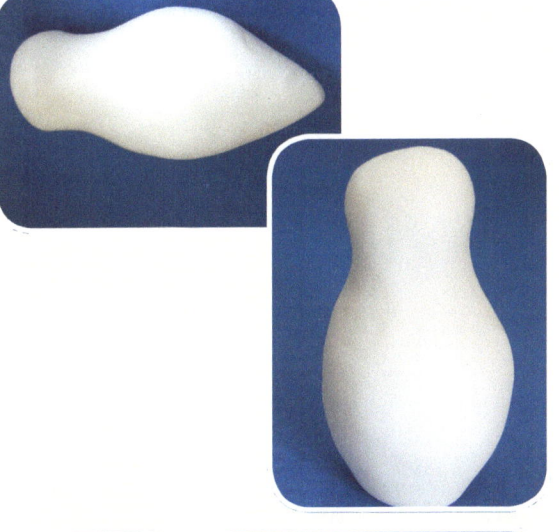

Tummy
Use a paper or cardboard template to keep the tummy white while spraying the rest of the model black.

After spraying allow to dry completely.

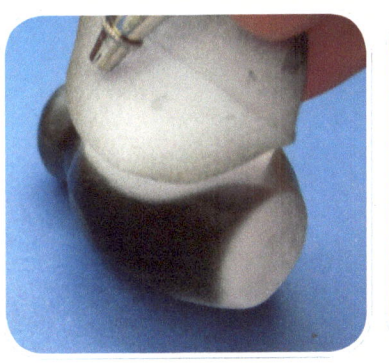

Beak

Make a tear drop, cut with scissors to make the mouth and shape the upper beak to be longer and slightly curved on the end.

Feet

Thinly roll out a piece of pale pink modelling paste. Using a plain cookie cutter cut out two discs of icing. Next use a slightly smaller cutter to make the shape as in the photograph and trim the centre part of the shape with a knife. Attach as feet using Tylose.

Fairy wings

From the same coloured paste used for the feet use a butterfly cutter to cut out the wings. Then cut in half and prop up so that they set curved.

Place the wings onto Styrofoam to dry completely.

Spray

Spray the fairy wings, feet and beak with a slightly deeper pink.

Penguin wings

Cut out two boat shaped wings from pale pink modelling paste and prop up so that they set curved. When set spray one side black and attach to the body.

Attaching feet

Attach the body to the feet with Tylose glue.

A small amount of modelling paste may be needed to prop up the model from the rear.

Attach beak
Cut the rear of the beak to make it flat and using Tylose glue to stick it to the head.

Eyebrows
Make two small sausage shapes of white modelling paste and attach them to the head with Tylose glue.

Fairy wings
Attach the fairy wings using Tylose glue.

Fairy sand castle.
Make the shapes as in the photograph.

Spray the castle and paint with a brush if you wish.

Finishing Touches

Spread some royal icing to act as glue then cover with cornmeal or sieved dry RTR to represent sand.

Attach the castle at the rear of the arrangement and arrange the penguins at the front.

I've attached a wired star and given the star and the buildings a sparkle with cornmeal but you could use coloured caster sugar.

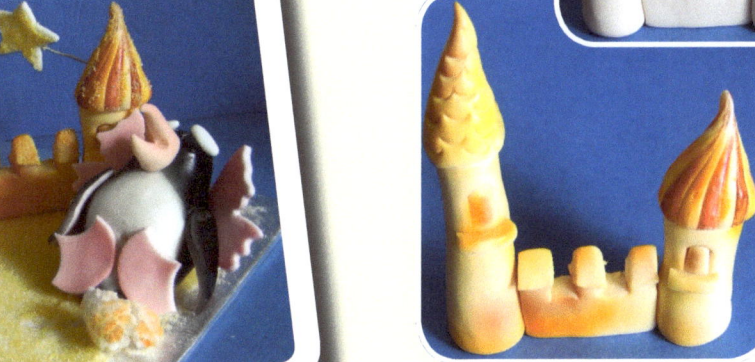

Koalas
...some party animal!

Sleep all day; play all night – some party animal! No wonder they always look so tired.

PART	WEIGHT	COLOUR
Body	50g	White
Head	30g	White
Ears	2 x 2g	White
Nose	1g	Black
Arms	2 x 10g	White
Box		Yellow
Bottle	25g	White
Cup cake	25g	Brown

Body
This body requires little shaping as it is hidden inside the box.

First shape the paste into a smooth ball.

Then use a Perspex modelling plate to make a cone shape with the narrow end being flat and the top end being slightly rounded.

Head
First shape the paste into a smooth ball then pinch with your finger and thumb to make the bridge of the nose.

Nose
Attach the black nose.

Mouth
Cut the mouth with a knife.

Forming the mouth
Next form the mouth with a dog bone tool.

Eye sockets and ears
Using a dog bone tool press in the indents for the eyes.

Using sticky modelling paste form spiky tear drop shapes and attach them to the head.

Arms and hands
Make two arms with hands and give them four spiky fingers.

Lightly spray all the body pieces grey.

Bottle
Shape the bottle with a Perspex modelling plate, shape the neck and attach a band around the end of the neck.

Finishing the bottle
After drying spray with green colour and a little brown. Finally attach a label and a medallion on the neck.

The finishing touch is a small piece of rock sugar attached to the neck of the bottle to resemble the bubbly shooting out of it.

Box
Cut out five squares of thin paste and five rectangles the same width but only half the depth. Set aside on Styrofoam to dry.

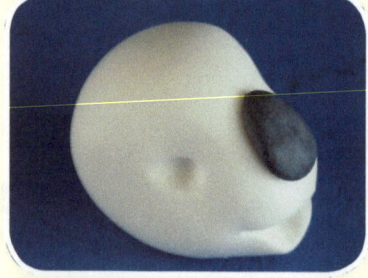

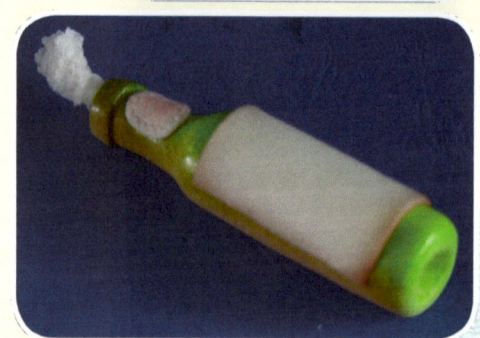

Assembling the box
When dry assemble using one of the squares as the base. Use royal icing to stick it together then allow it to dry completely.

Decorating the box
Add a star to each side.

Flaps of the box
The flaps for the box are first sprayed and allowed to dry then they are stuck onto the top edge of the box with royal icing and propped up while they dry.

Cupcake
Using pale grey paste shape as a cork and mark grooves around the side. Cut out a large blossom and attach it to the top. Press the ball tool into each petal of the flower and make an indent in the centre.

To finish the cupcake
Spray the blossom on top of the cup cake, make a candle and flame and attach in the centre of the cup cake. A small rose bud has also been added.

Streamers
Thinly roll out some modelling paste and cut into narrow strips, then twist and allow dry.

Finishing Touches.
Position the box.
Place the body in the box – use royal icing to hold it in place.
Attach the head, pipe in the eyes with royal icing and chocolate.
Attach the arms and bottle with Tylose then position the streamers.
Last of all add the cupcake.

Kookaburras
...happy chappies with their hearty laugh.

It doesn't matter whether the jokes are good or bad these happy chappies just have to show their appreciation with their hearty laugh.

PART	WEIGHT	COLOUR
Body	50g	Cream
Beak	5g	Brown
Tongue	1g	Pink
Wings	Various	Brown
Feet	2g x 2	Yellow

Body
Make a pear shape.

Make the markings across the front.

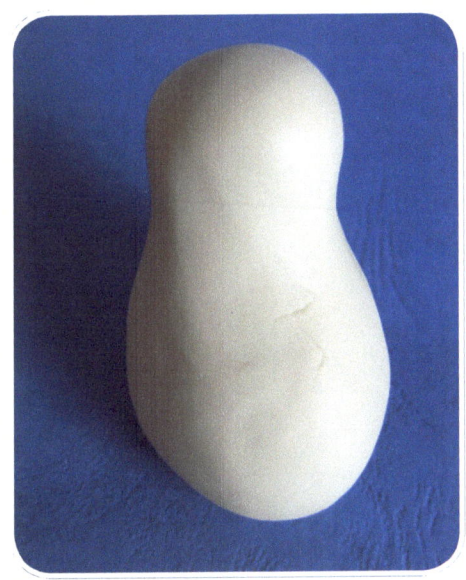

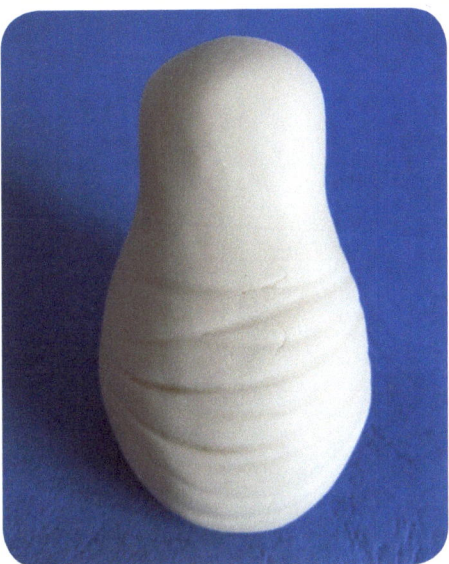

Beak

Make a tear drop, cut it with a pair of scissors, hollow the inside and make two holes for nostrils on the top. Add two small balls of modelling paste to the sides and attach a small pink tear drop that has been flattened and grooved down its centre for its tongue.

Attaching the beak

Attach the beak to the body with Tylose glue.

Claws

Make the claws by making three pointed tear drops (very small) then place them together to make the claw.

Spray

Spray the body around the back and along the lower part at the front.

Attach the claws.

Wings

Roll out some modelling paste and cut out with a large rose leaf cutter.

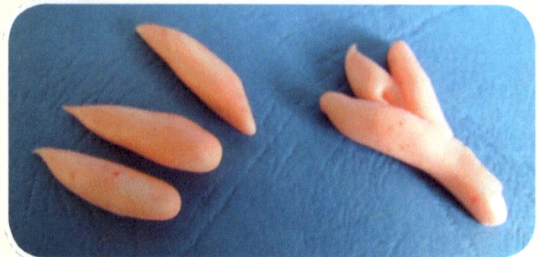

Cut out more rose leaves with the smallest cutter and starting at the pointed end of the large shape start attaching the smaller ones with Tylose, working backwards from the point. Spray.

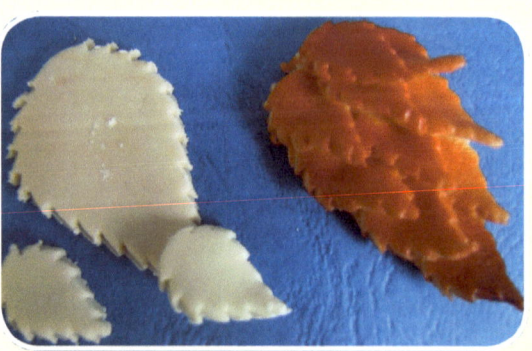

Tail

Roll out some modelling paste and cut out as in the picture. I used a round cutter to round off the edge.

Mark the feathers in with a modelling tool then spray.

Tree stump

Fashion some modelling paste into a rough tree stump make an indent in the centre for the bird to sit in. Spray then attach the bird's tail using Tylose.

Finishing Touches

Attach the wings to the body.

Make a slouch hat and set it in place.

Add a tree, marbled stone and blossom with a leaf.

Octopus
...great at finding treasure

This old pirate is a friend of Jack Sparrow's and is great at finding treasure. Having eight arms also means he can carry more away while fighting off his enemies.

PART	WEIGHT	COLOUR
Body	15g	Grey
Head	45g	Grey
Tentacles	15g x 4	Grey
Hat	10 (centre ball)	Black
Treasure chest	50g	Brown
Patch, moustache and beard		Black

Head

Shape the head as an egg shape.

Using the bone tool make an eye socket.

The mouth is made by inserting the small bone tool and pulling it in a downward direction.

Attach an ear and a black patch using Tylose.

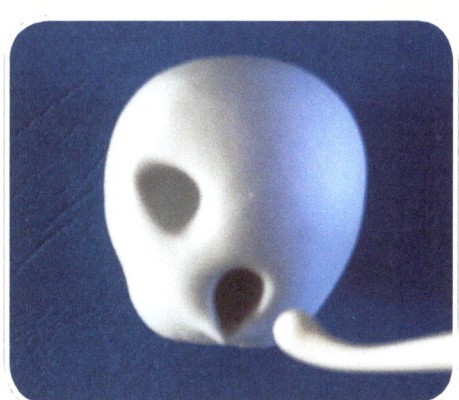

Tentacles
Make four cigar shapes.

Using the bone tool make indents to represent the suckers.

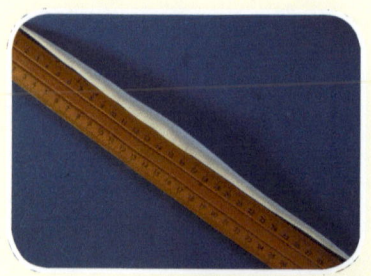

Treasure chest
Shape two pieces of modelling paste, one into a block for the base of the chest and a curved piece for the lid.

Mark with a modelling tool to represent planks of wood.

Spray the pieces and set aside to dry.

Adding the treasure
Set the chest in place and arrange foil covered chocolate coins around it and make treasure from modelling paste.

Arranging the tentacles
Assemble the tentacles around and over the treasure.

Hat

Make a pirate's tricorn hat by cutting out a thin circle of paste, place a ball in the centre and arrange the circle to form three sides.

Spray it black and leave it to dry then attach a skull and cross bones and a white feather.

Assembly

Make a frill to sit on top of the tentacles.

Attach the head and the hat.

Make an earring and attach it to the ear.

Finishing Touches

Add a nose, moustache and beard.

Pipe in the eye with royal icing and chocolate.

Place a dagger in one tentacle, a bottle of rum in another and one can be holding a gold coin.

Parrot
...really do squawk a lot....

So pretty but the females really do squawk a lot – but what's new?

PART	WEIGHT	COLOUR
Body and head	70g	Wedgewood blue
Eye sockets	1g x 2	Wedgewood blue
Wings	3g x 2	Wedgewood blue
Tail	4g x 3	White
Beak	4g	Orange
Feet	1g x 2	Pale brown
Tree stump	40g	Dark brown

Body and head
Using Wedgewood blue coloured paste shape the body as a dumbbell with one end larger than the other.

Make the markings on the breast of the bird with the curved tool.

Eyes
Make two balls for eye sockets and press into position with the bone tool.

Beak
Make the beak by shaping a cone shape marking the opening and bending the shape downwards.

Attach the beak and make two nostril holes.

Wings

Cut two wings using the largest rose leaf cutter (plain side).

Next emboss with a leaf veiner to represent the feathers.

Colouring

After attaching the wings with tylose, spray around the eye sockets (note that I have made markings around the eyes).

Spray the wings with a deeper blue on the tips.

Spray the beak with a deeper orange.

Plume

Attach a plume of white to the head (made by pressing white icing through a fine sieve/sifter or tea strainer).

Tree stump

With white or pale brown paste make a thickish rope.

Score it to represent the bark of a tree.

Spray it to give it some depth.

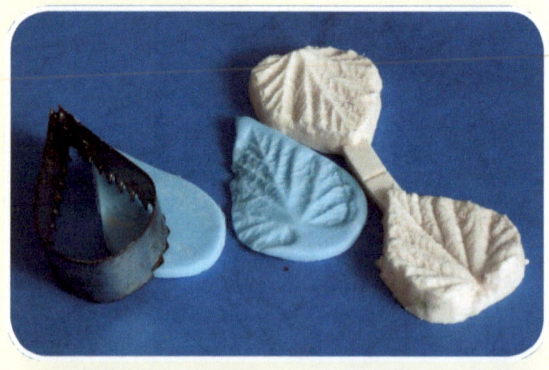

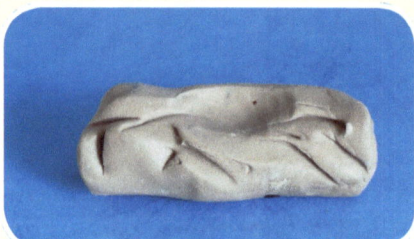

Tail

For the tail make three long tear drops and roll out thin with a rolling pin.

Cut one end into a point and shape over a rolling pin until completely dry. (add some CMC powder to help set them hard).

Claws

Make the claws from three tiny cones and squeeze together then bend downwards.

Finishing Touches

Set the parrot onto the tree stump attach the claws and the tail using Tylose. Spray the tips of the claws with pale brown.

Add a large blossom and a speckled egg.

Pipe in the whites of the eyes with royal icing and finish with chocolate.

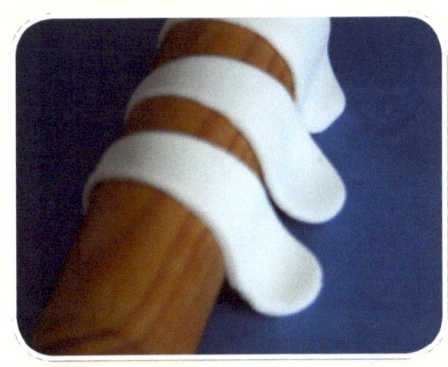

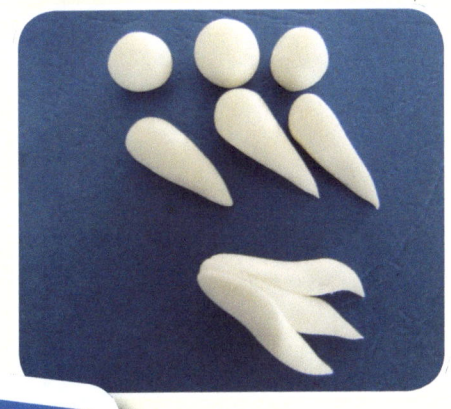

Platypus
What a Heinz 57 variety!

What a Heinz 57 variety! The Creator must have either had a bad day or had run out of ideas so He put a few bits and pieces together from previous creations and left it up to others to guess its name.

This elegant fellow is the mayor of Latrobe in Tasmania's north, which, as everyone knows is the capital of platypus land.

PART	WEIGHT	COLOUR
Body and head	45g	Pale brown with a touch of black
Bill	2g	Pale brown
Legs	7g	Pale brown with a touch of black
Arms	3g	Pale brown with a touch of black
Tail	12g	Pale yellow with a touch of black
Hat	12g	Black

Body
First model the body, making it elongated.

Legs and feet
Form the legs and feet.

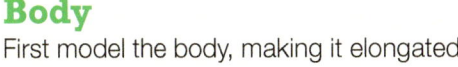

Arms and hands
Shape the arms and hands.

Spray
Spray the parts with black colour so that they are grey.

Next attach the bill, eye sockets shirt front and bow tie using Tylose.

Arms and tail
Attach the arms.

Make the tail, spray it grey and attach it to the body.

Use Tylose to glue both.

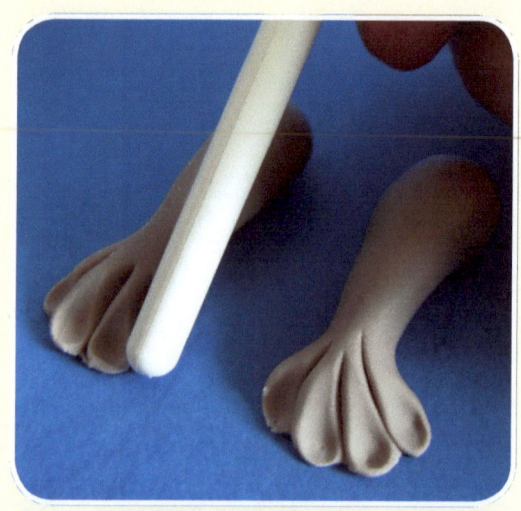

Finishing Touches

Pipe in the whites of the eyes with royal icing and finish with chocolate.

Attach some white hair and attach it to the head.

Make a top hat with a band and a small blossom and put in place with Tylose.

Add a few stones, a bit of grass and a nest with eggs in it and eh voila you have the perfect habitat.

Possum
...a tail that doubles as a scarf.

Winter is the ideal time for all cool dudes to wrap up warm and what better than a tail that doubles as a scarf. To ward off colds and flu he gets his vitamin C from the gardens and alleys he visits.

PART	WEIGHT	COLOUR
Body	50g	Brown
Belly	5g	White
Head	15g	Brown
Face	2g	White
Tail	12g	Brown
Legs	7g x 2	Brown
Arm	7g x 2	Brown
Nose		Dark brown
Garbage bin base	65g	White
Outside strip of bin	35g	White
Bin lid	20g	White
Orange slice	20g	White

Body
Model the body into a pear shape and make an indent for the tummy.

Tummy
Mould the tummy and press it flat before attaching it to the body. Make a belly button with the cone tool.

Legs
Shape the leg and foot as a bone shape and press flat then mark the toes.

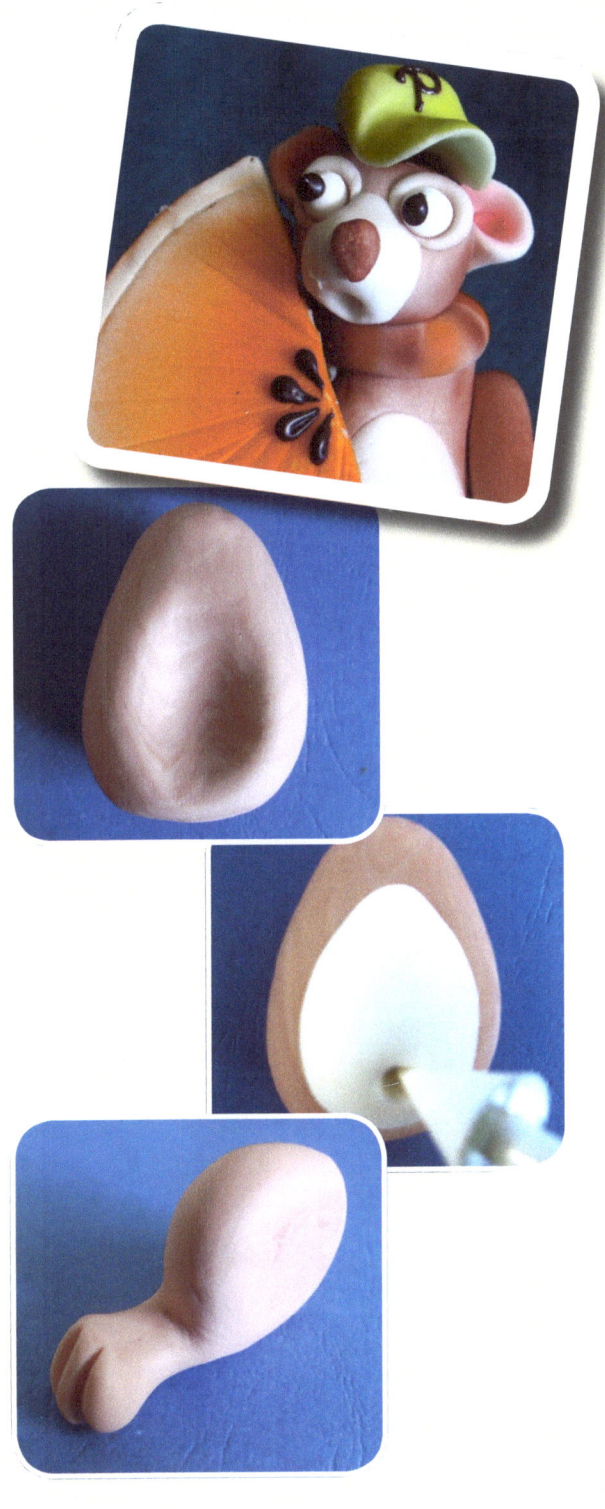

59

Attaching legs
Attach the legs to the body using Tylose.

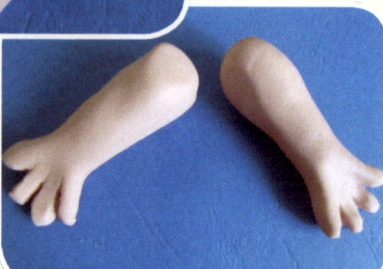

Arms
Make the arms and hands as a dumbbell shape. Thin one end of the arm, cut the fingers and round off the finger shapes.

Attach the left arm to the body using tylose.

Tail
Make a long rope and attach it to the back of the model, bring it up and curl it around where the neck would be and down to the hand on the left hand side.

Spray the model with brown colour taking care not to spray colour onto the white belly. Now spray orange bands to make the tail striped and paint on black lines.

Head
Make the head as a ball and attach the muzzle. Press in two balls of white modelling paste for the eye sockets.

Attach two circles of paste for the ears and a nose.

Attach the head to the body.

Orange slice
Roll out some white modelling paste and taper it. Cut out a part circle and trim the tapered edge.

Mark an inner circle with the back of a smaller cutter.

Make the markings on the centre section.

Spray the centre and the edge by protecting the white parts with the cutters. When dry attach the slice to the body and the right arm around the slice using Tylose.

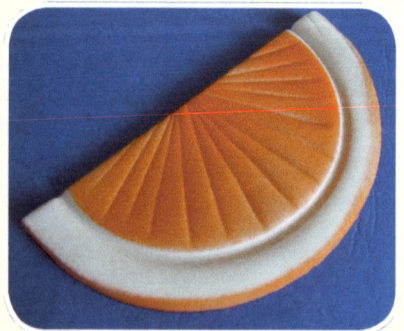

Garbage bin

Make a cylinder shape and set on one side.

Roll out some paste and cut a strip the same width as the height of the cylinder, at the same time cut three narrow strips.

Wet the cylinder and roll it over the largest strip.

Sides of bin

Moisten two of the narrow strips and attach one to the top and one to the bottom edge.

Using the bone tool mark the grooves in the side of the garbage bin.

Handles

From the third narrow strip make three handles, two for the sides of the bin and one for the lid.

Lid

Make a ball and press it down with the palm of your hand. Next make the marks in the lid with the bone tool.

Attach the handle to the lid. Mark the rivets with a number three plain piping tube.

Spray

Spray the garbage bin with black colour.

Finishing Touches

Finally assemble with some small fruits and vegies with leaves.

Roo
and little Joey

Wow! Little Joey is such a hungry little 'un' mum has to resort to the bottle so that he'll grow up to be a healthy, bouncy boy.

PART	WEIGHT	COLOUR
Body	50g	Brown
Head	12g	Brown
Ears	1g ÷ 2	Brown
Tail	10g	Brown
Thighs	6g x 2	Brown
Feet	2g each	Brown
Arm	5g x 2	Brown
Joey	2g	Brown
Hair		White
Baby Bottle	15g	White
Pinafore		Peach
Nose		Dark brown

Body
Make as a pear shape.

Tail
Shape as a long tear-drop and flatten the broad end.

Brush with Tylose solution and place the body on top of it. Shape so that it is bending upwards.

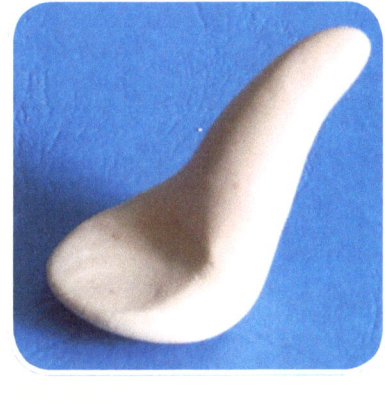
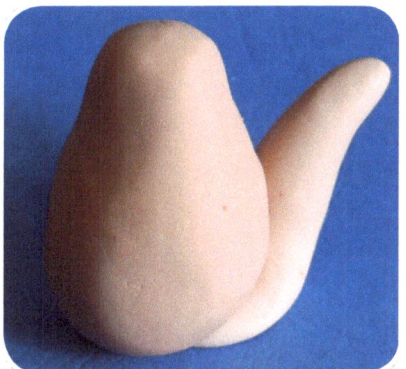

63

Head

Shape as tear-drop with a slightly rounder end. Flatten the tapered end slightly. Cut the mouth with small knife and shape the opening with a bone shaped modelling tool. Make the cheeks with a curved modelling tool.

Ears

Make 2 small tear drop shapes. Moisten the broader ends with Tylose solution. Using the bone tool press the ears onto the head. Attach a small tear drop for the nose.

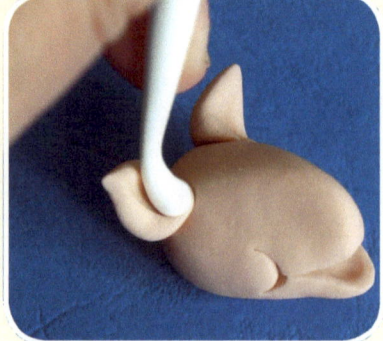

Thighs

Mould two tear-drops and lengthen slightly.

Brush one side of the wider end with Tylose and place against the body sloping backwards at approx 45°, press firmly without distorting the shapes.

Feet

Shape as for the thighs and mark with 2 grooves at the wider end. Brush the tapered ends with Tylose solution and place at the bottom of the thighs.

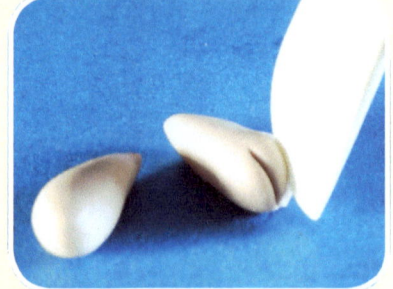

Arms and hands

Make as pears but elongate and elongate the centre of the shape so that it has a smaller ball at one end then a thinner area (wrist) with the rest gradually widening to form the shoulder.

Flatten the ball slightly and cut 3 times with scissors to form the fingers. Bend the arms slightly in the centre and mark creases.

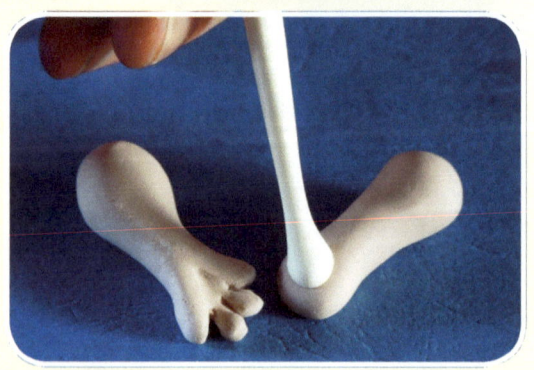

64

Bottle

The bottle is made from a sausage of paste. At one end a disc of pink icing is added and marked with grooves. Using the cone tool make an indent in the pink disc. Make a tear drop of pale pink paste and attach it in the indent, this is the teat.

Finally make the markings on the bottle with a food grade marker.

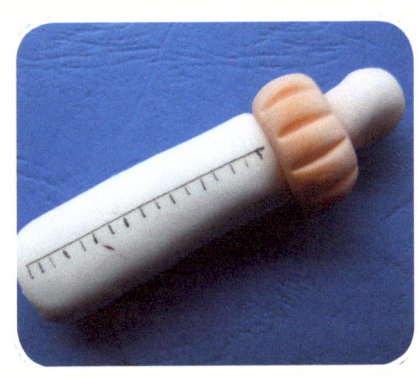

Assembly

Assemble as in the picture using Tylose glue.

Spray

Spray carefully with slightly darker brown to resemble fur.

Finishing Touches

Add the hair which is a flattened tear drop topped with a blossom. Pipe in the eyes with royal icing and chocolate and they're finished.

Accessories include a stone of marbled grey paste, grass made by pressing green paste through a sieve/sifter and a blossom and leaf. In this picture I have added a pinafore.

Seagulls
...mine, mine, mine...

We love our take-away which ever brand it might be. But remember it's mine, mine, mine so get your own!

PART	WEIGHT	COLOUR
Body, neck and head	60g	White
Beak	20g	Orange
Eye balls	2g x 2	White
Wings	12g x 2	Grey
Tail	9g	Grey
Feet	16g x 2	Orange
Burger bun	65g	Cream
Burger patty	50g	Brown
French fries	4g x 12	Cream
Lettuce leaves		Green
Tomato		Red
Wrapping paper		White

Body and head

These are made from one piece of modelling paste. After moulding the paste round and making it smooth form it into a type of dumbbell shape with a larger proportion at the bottom for the body, elongate the rest to make the neck and the head. Make the rear of the body pointed.

Beak

Initially shape the beak as a tear drop. Cut the mouth with a pair of scissors and make two indents with a pointed tool or the one in the photo for the nostrils.

Attach the beak to the head and support it until set.

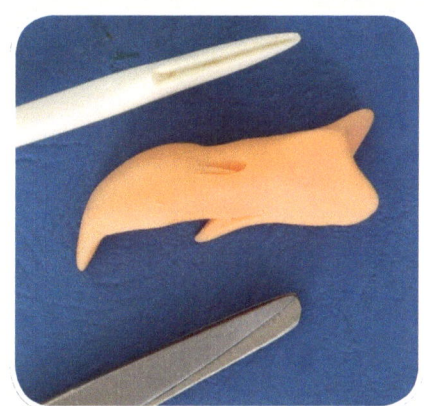

Eyes
Make two eye balls and attach above the beak. Add a feather or two to the head.

Wings
Make two grey tear drops and flatten then mark the feathers with a modelling tool. Spray the lower edge and the tips with a darker grey/black. Attach to the body when dry using Tylose.

Tail
Make a smaller tear drop than the wings and flatten it making it into a fan. Mark the feathers with the same tool as the one used for the wings. Spray the top edge with a darker grey / black. Attach to the body. Support until set. Attach to the body with Tylose and support it until it sets.

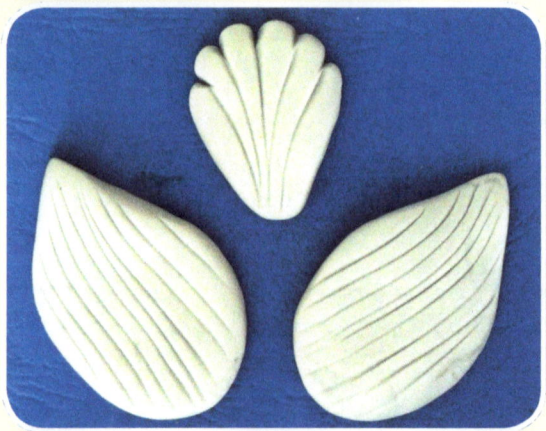

Feet
Make the feet as in the photo using the cone shaped tool to make the webs between the toes.

Burger
Make a ball of paste and shape as a burger bun. Next cut it through. Take some small pieces of the same coloured paste and shape as sesame seeds.

Using darker modelling paste shape the beef patty and texturize.

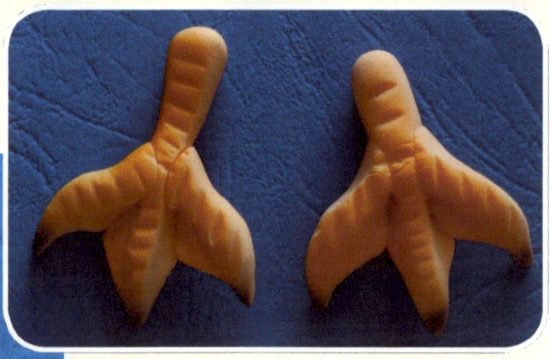

Lettuce

Roll out some green modelling paste and make lettuce leaves from it. Spray with a deeper green and a little brown.

French fries

Make fries from some more paste by rolling it out to the desired thickness then cutting strips. Then spray a golden brown.

Finishing Touches

Spray all the parts and assemble on a sheet of white modelling paste. Paint on the eyes or pipe them with dark chocolate.

Sheep
...*dear little lambs always look so smart*...

Baabara loves to knit woolly jumpers for her lambs. Knit one pearl one, all day long. Her dear little lambs always look so smart in their new outfits.

PART	WEIGHT	COLOUR
Body	60g	White
Face	7g	Black
Legs	14g ÷ 4	Black
Tape	g	Yellow
Knitting pins	9g ÷ 2	Brown

Parts to dry
Make the legs, rods and knitting needle tops a day or so before and allow them to dry out.

Body
Make a ball of white modelling paste and make four indents on the base to take the legs and two holes in the top to take the knitting needles. Attach the legs.

Head
Make the head by shaping a tear drop and attaching the ears to the narrow end. Make the eye sockets with a small bone tool and the mouth with the curved tool. Make some hair by pressing modelling paste through a sieve.

Finishing Touches

Add a tape measure, some grass and a wooly-pully (pull over/jumper).
Attach the head and place the knitting pins into the holes.
Pipe in the eyes with royal icing and chocolate.
Finally press some paste through a fine sieve/sifter and attach for the hair.

Accessories
A thin strip of paste rolled up at one end and marked as a tape measure some grass made in the same way as the hair and a rectangle of paste to represent the knitting.

71

Soldier Crabs
Neptune's choice for the regal guard…

This tiny crab is Neptune's choice for the regal guard and is drawn from Victorian, Queensland and Tasmanian brigades. In their smart blue uniform they keep watch as sentries at Neptune's Palace only to quickly burrow into the sand when the enemy approaches. Ah-tehn-shun no slacking on parade Neptune is on his way.

PART	WEIGHT	COLOUR
Shell	50g	Beige
Lower shell	15g	Beige
Claws	2 x 20g	Beige
Legs	8 x 10g	Beige
Hat	30g	Blue
Coral and sand	Made from 'Rock Sugar' and sprayed with an airbrush	

Body

Shape as a ball and make into an egg shape.

Flatten the tapered end.

Using a rose leaf cutter make a marking on the flat side of the shell.

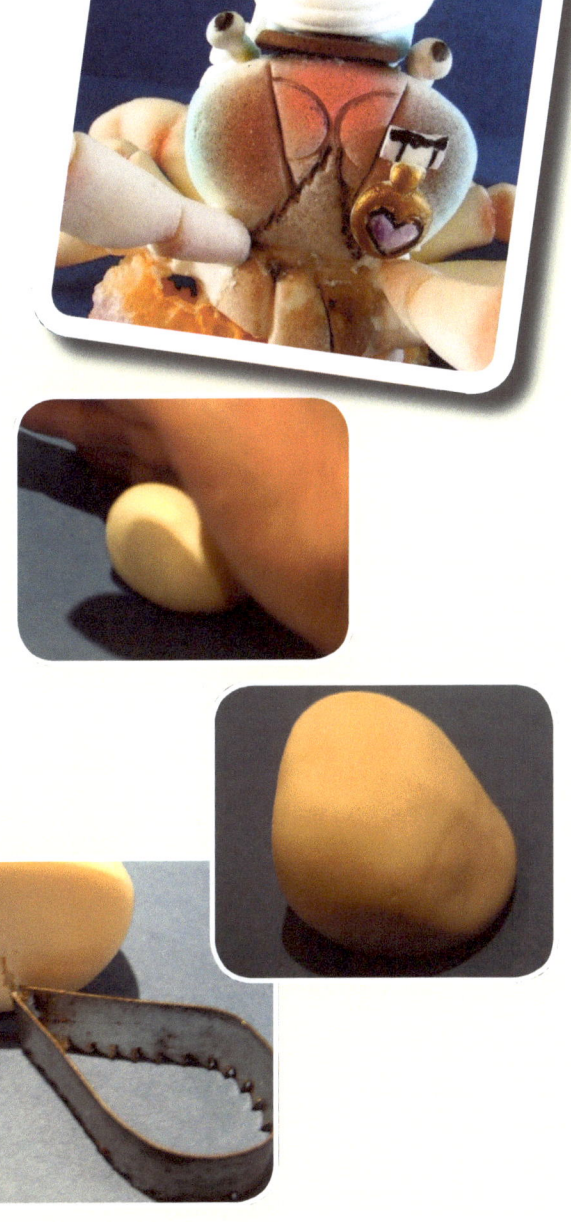

Legs

Shape the leg as a cigar type shape (see photo- one end tapered and the other narrow with a thicker part in the middle).

Using the modelling tool in the photo hold it at an angle and make the markings on each leg – set aside to dry completely.

Claws

Shape the claws as a cone shape and using your fingers model in the shape as in the photo.

Using the same technique used for the legs mark in the joints on the claw.

Next cut the broad end to make the claw with a knife and mark in the serrations with the same modelling tool you used to mark the joints in the legs and claws.

Set aside to dry completely.

This is what it looks like but without the hat.

The stalks for the eyes must be attached before the next step.

Spray

Spray the shell blue around the back and down the sides.

Spray a little pale pink (watered down red) in the centre of the face and a little pale brown either side.

Paint the eyes on the end of the stalks.

Under shell

Make a ball and press it flat making three markings.

Spray with a little pink at the front and pale brown at the sides.

Attach the shell to the under shell using Tylose.

Spray

The claws and legs are sprayed and the parts now look like this. The tips of the claws and the legs are sprayed black).

The legs are attached to the under shell and are supported until set (I used royal icing to attach the legs).

Support the pieces

The claws are also attached with royal icing and supported until set.

The crab is adorned with a medal for bravery and is finished with his ceremonial hat.

Seaweed and seahorses

Some seaweed is made from green modelling paste cut as long thin triangles, sprayed a deeper green and sea horses moulded from a silicon mould are attached.

Finishing Touches

Add coral made from rock sugar (see rear of the book) which is sprayed with food dye.

The crab is supported on a small piece of coral and some sea plants are added too.

Tassie Devil
...just like Ned Kelly

Out in the Tasmanian bush the bush rangers hid. This little Devil wants to be one too and is collecting his tools of the trade so he can be just like Ned Kelly.

PART	WEIGHT	COLOUR
Body	100g	White
Head	70g	White
Legs	115g	Burgundy
Boots	8g	Brown
Arms	15g	White
Hat	30g	Brown
Helmet	150g	White
Gun	115g	White
Wanted Poster	120g	White

Legs
Colour the modelling paste and roll out as a sausage shape.

Fold over and bend twice so that the model is sitting.

Mark in the creases and place onto a raised surface to dry.

Head
Mould round then pinch the snout, mark in the eye sockets, cut the mouth and open it up.

Make two small cones and attach as ears.

Body
Shape the body with a slightly tapered base (the model's waist).

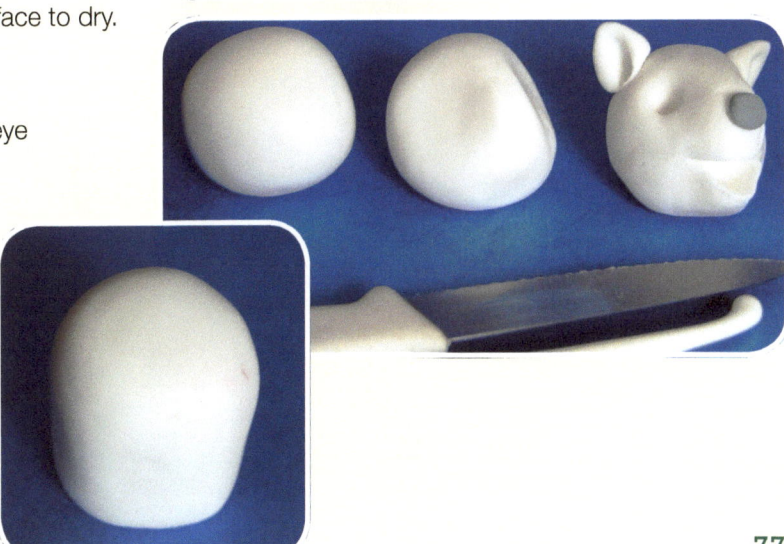

Ned Kelly's helmet
Shape the hat and mark in the seams, rivets and opening. The rivets are marked with a number three piping tube/tip.

Ned Kelly's gun
Shape the gun and spray.

Finished gun
After spraying on one side allow to dry, turn over and spray the other side.

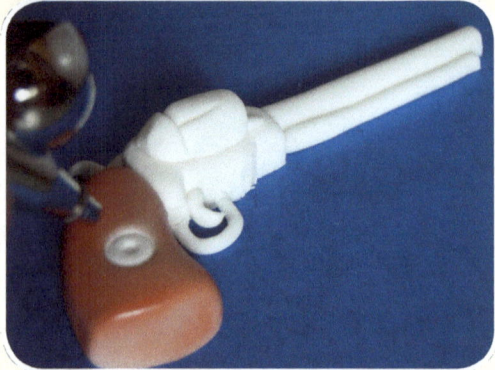

Assembling the body
Make the shoes and attach using a small amount of RTR with a teaspoon of water that is melted in the microwave(Caution this will burn if you get it on your fingers).

Make a band of modelling paste and wrap it around the body folding the top corners over so that it looks like a waist coat.

Spray it brown.

Make a narrow strip of paste, spray it a darker brown, allow to dry: then wrap around the model's waist.

Form a buckle and attach it.

Finally add a scarf by cutting a triangle of paste and add a patch to one knee.

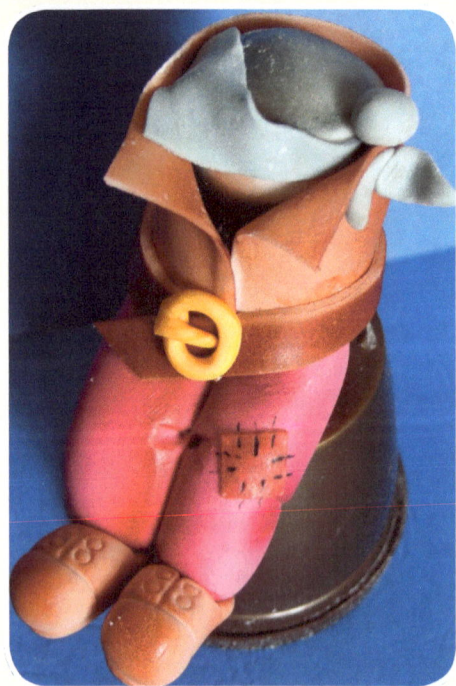

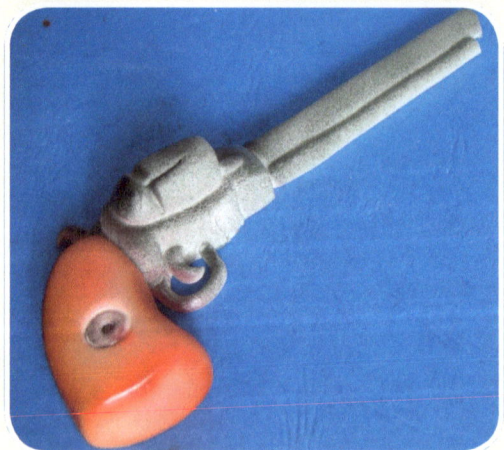

78

Spray the head

After spaying the head with black spray inside the ears and mouth with pink and add two lower teeth.

Spray helmet

Spray the helmet with black to produce a metalic look.

Hat

Make the hat and spray light brown.

Add the rope and the skull.

Finishing Touches

Sit the body onto the helmet.

Attach the head and put the hat in place adding a small amount of hair made as a tear drop, flattened and mark with a modelling tool.

Pipe in the eyes with royal icing and chocolate.

Attach the gun.

Finally add some fencing and a rock or two and position the wanted poster.

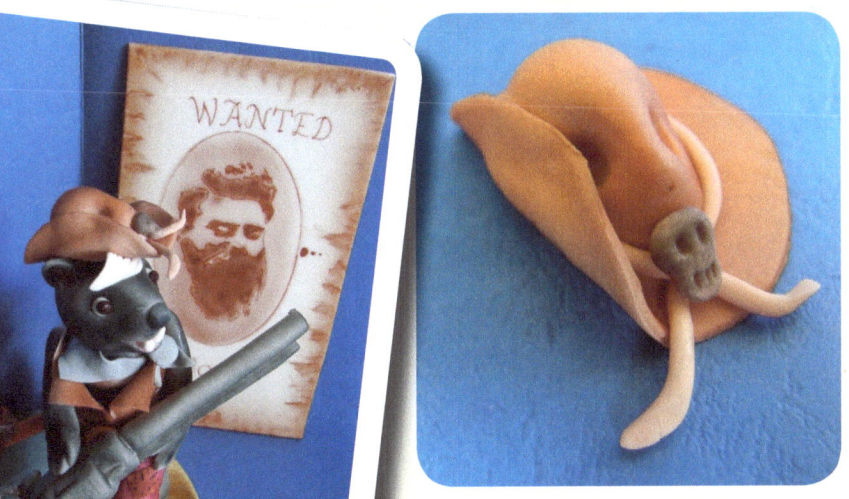

Tree Frog
…like a Guru, meditates all day…

Croak is probably the most colourful character in the rain-forest. He sits in his tree and, like a Guru, meditates all day while waiting for his food to come to him. Damn it's way past feeding time – where's my grub, or dragon fly or mozzie?

PART	WEIGHT	COLOUR
Body	40g	Green
Head	17g	Green
Eyebrows	2g ÷ 2	Green
legs	7g x 2	Green
Feet	5g x 2	Green
Hands	2g	Green
Arms	3g	Green

Body
Make the body as a pear shape positioning it so that it lies back a little.

Feet and legs

Make the feet and the legs.

Making the feet

The feet are made from four strands of modelling paste which are moulded together at one end.

Next the small balls are attached using Tylose.

Attaching the legs and feet

Put the legs in place and attach the feet using Tylose to glue them in place.

Head

To make the head make a pear shape and flatten the broad end while leaving the narrow end upright.

Cut the mouth with a knife and shape the opening with a small bone tool.

Attach two small balls for the eyes, pressing in with the bone tool. Make two indents for the nostrils.

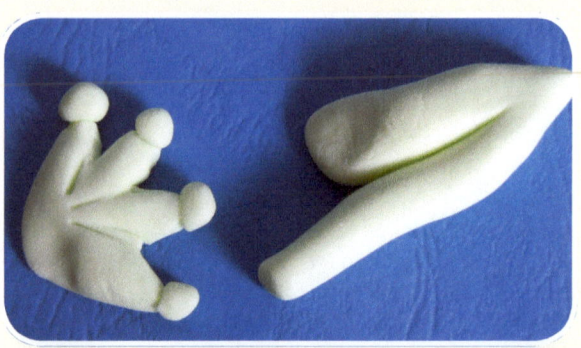

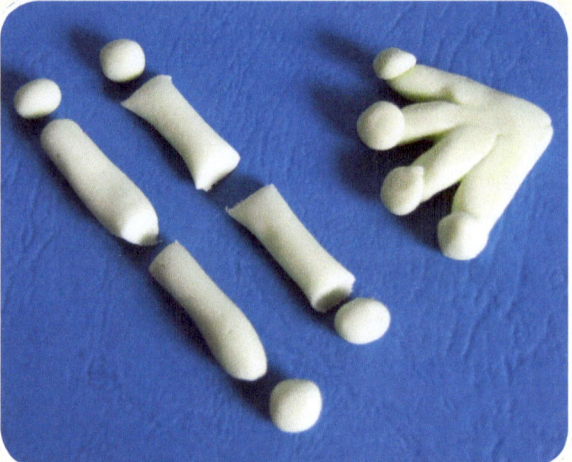

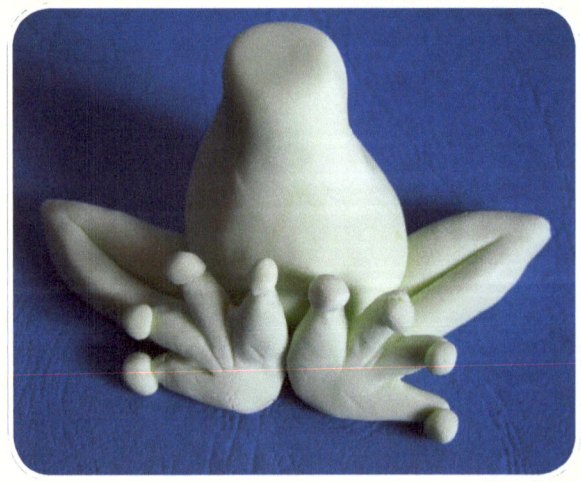

Assemble

Attach the head to the body and two arms and hands (made in the same way as the feet) using Tylose to stick them.

Finishing Touches

Spray the model a deeper green.

Spray a little pink in the mouth and around the eyes.

Pipe in the eyes with royal icing and chocolate.

Add an exotic orchid from the rain forest and he's finished but still no grub, dragonfly or mozzie!

Turtles
...move to the rhythm of their own drum.

Here's a little secret – turtles are very musical and they all move to the rhythm of their own drum.

PART	WEIGHT	COLOUR
Body	45g	Pale green
Tummy	3g	White
Head	8g	Flesh
Eyes	1g ÷ 2	Flesh
Legs	2 x 4g	Flesh
Arms	2 x 5g	Flesh
Drum sticks	1g x 2	Brown
Bow tie		Red

Shell

Make a ball of pale green icing into the shell by pressing it down onto the table top to make a flat surface. Next press down into the icing with one finger to make the markings.

Turn up the other way and make sure the model sits straight.

Tummy
Roll out some white icing and cut out a circle to cover the top surface of the shell.

Arms
Form the arms and hands as in the picture.

Feet
Shape the legs and feet from one piece of paste and mark the toes with a bone tool.

Head
Shape the head as a pear shape and form a neck out of the bigger end. Cut a mouth with a knife, make two small holes for nostrils then mark the neck. Next attach two eye sockets and some strands of hair using Tylose as glue.

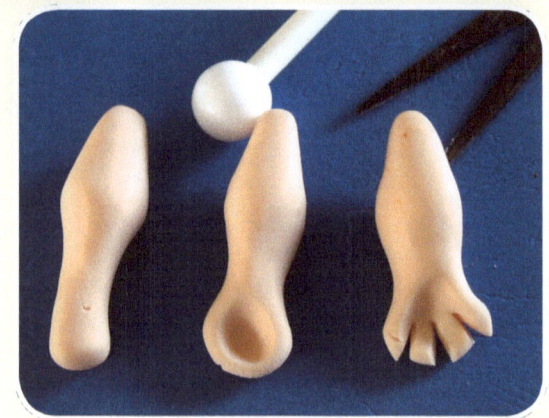

Spray the parts
Shell – green and brown.

Arms, legs and head - flesh colour.

Assemble
Make a rope and attach it around the top edge of the shell. Attach the head, arms and legs. Use Tylose glue to stick the parts together.

Finishing Touches
Add the drum sticks, make a bow tie and pipe in the eyes with royal icing and chocolate.

Finally give the turtle some sheet music to play to.

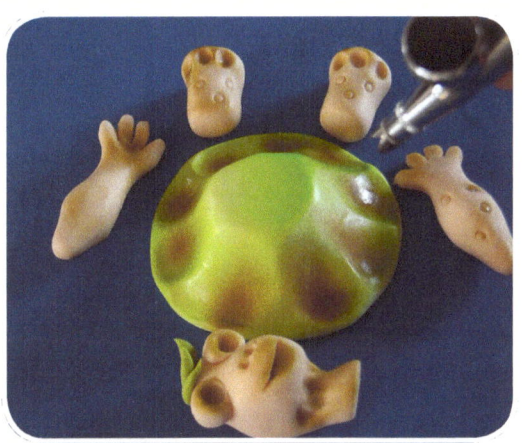

Wabbits
...cute little furry bunnies...

The Easter bunny may not be visiting Western Australia this year – it seems that the government doesn't like cute little furry bunnies with lots of chockies.

PART	WEIGHT	COLOUR
Body	40g	Brown
Head	20g	Brown
Eyebrows	2g ÷ 2	Brown
Ears		Brown
Cheeks		Pale brown
legs	3g x 2	Brown
Feet	7g x 2	Brown
Hand	5g	Brown
Carrot	12g	Orange
Carrot leaves	2g	Green
Hair		Orange
Teeth		White
Tail	1g	White
Nose		Black

Body
Make an egg shape.

Legs
Make two small cylinder shapes and attach to the body with Tylose.

Feet

Make the feet as two ovals and flatten one side on the table.

Mark in the toes using a modelling tool.

Attach to the legs with Tylose.

Hand

Make a hand in a similar way to the feet and attach it to the body again with Tylose.

Head

Make the head from another egg shape and make the eye sockets with a bone tool.

Cheeks

Attach two small egg shapes and flatten for his cheeks.

Make his whiskers with a pointed tool.

Eye brows

Attach two small cylinder shapes, flatten them and mark.

Ears

Roll out some modelling paste that is thin.

Using an orchid petal cutter cut out two shapes.

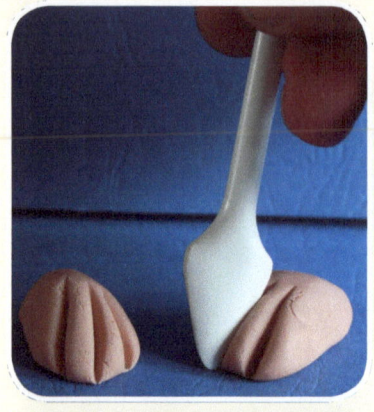
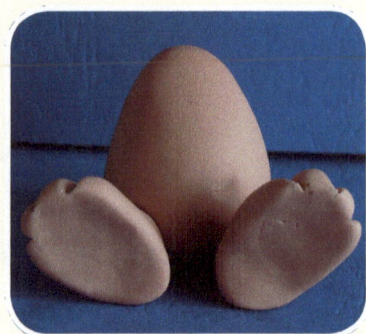

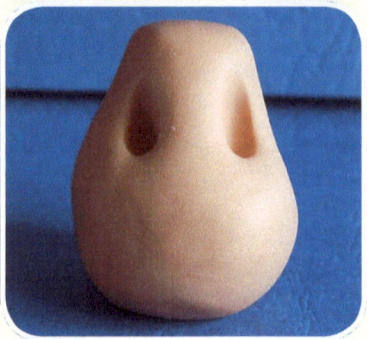
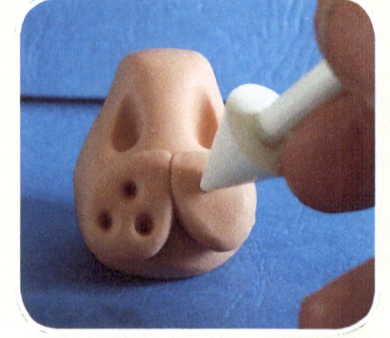
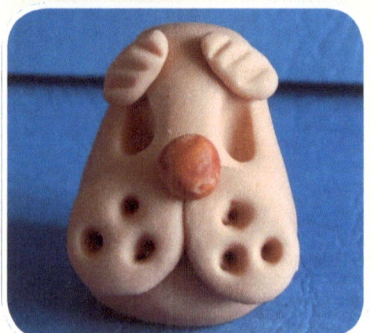
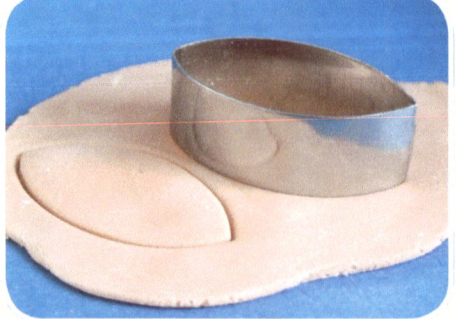

Positioning ears and nose

Attach the ears to the head.

Make a nose in a darker brown and put in place.

Assembly

Attach the head to the body with Tylose.

Spray with a darker brown.

Attach two goofy teeth and the hair.

Finishing Touches

Pipe in the eyes using royal icing and chocolate.

Add a carrot made from a cone of orange modelling paste sprayed deeper orange and add a bit of greenery.

In this arrangement I have added a nest with a couple of eggs and a daffodil. To tell the story I have added a poster and the rabbit proof fence.

Wombat
...wonderful chubby little fellas

These wonderful chubby little fellas are not so good at crossing roads but this one is on the mend. I'm sure the "Get Well Soon" card will help speed up his recovery.

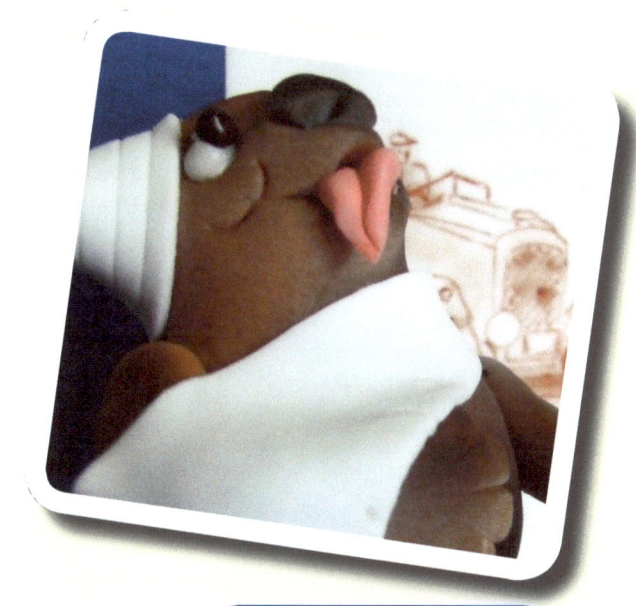

PART	WEIGHT	COLOUR
Body and head	150g	Grey
Legs and feet	2 x 12g	Grey
Nose		Black
Arms and hands	2 x 12g	Grey
Get well card	60g	White
Wheel	154g	White
Thermometer	20g	White

Body and Head

Make a ball first to get the modelling paste smooth. Make into a dumbbell shape.

Cut the mouth with a sharp knife.

Open the mouth with the bone tool.

Mark on the cheeks with the curved tool. Attach the nose.

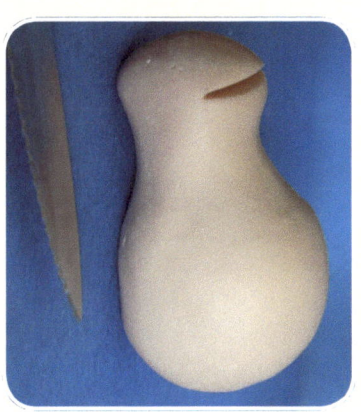 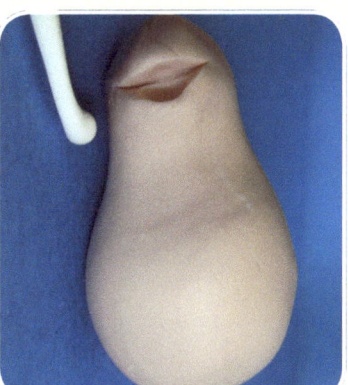 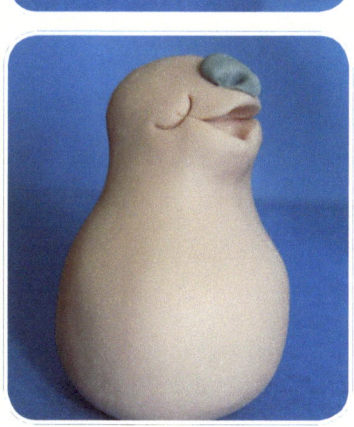

Legs
Shape as a sausage with a ball on the end.

Press to form the foot and mark the toes. This is done by holding the leg upwards and pressing the tool in to the foot

Arms
This is done in a similar way to the feet except the palm of the hand is shaped with the ball tool.

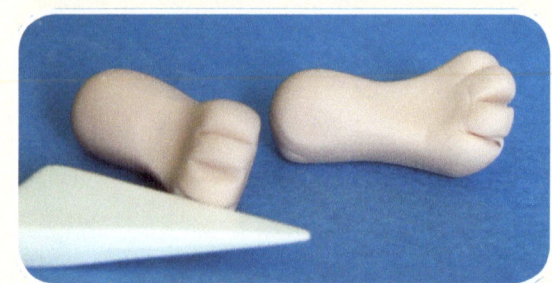

Spray
Spray the body with a darker brown.

Attach
Attach bandages to the head, and a sling to one of the arms.

The bandages are best made by making them as a broad band and marking them to look like several.

Assemble the legs
Stick the legs together after wrapping a bandage around one of the legs.

Sit the body of top of the legs sticking it with Tylose.

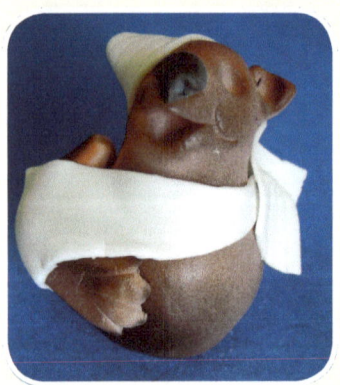 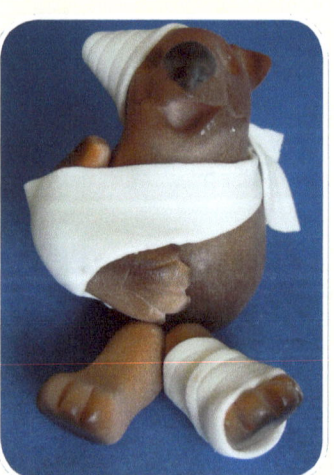

Thermometer

Shape the thermometer from white modelling paste and allow it to dry.

Paint the black line down the thermometer and make some marks for calibrations.

Paint the red bulb and line and set aside to dry.

Car tyre

First make a ball of modelling paste and fatten it.

Mark the wheel rim and hub cap with the back of two round cookie cutters.

Mark the tread on the edge of the tyre with the modelling tool.

Finally spray the tyre black and the rest red.

Finishing Touches

Sit the wombat on the tyre and attach the thermometer.

Pipe in the eyes with royal icing and chocolate.

Finally make the get well card and position it behind the model.

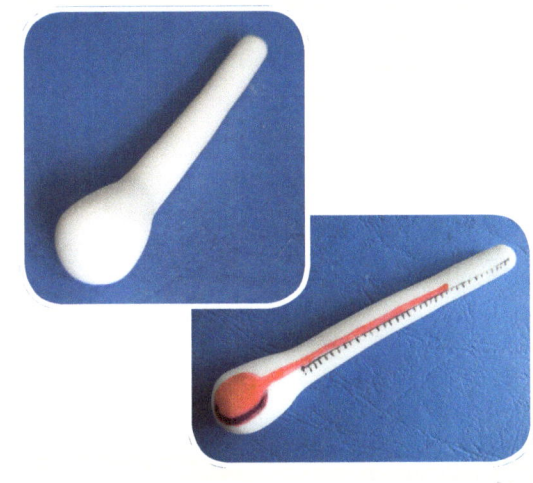
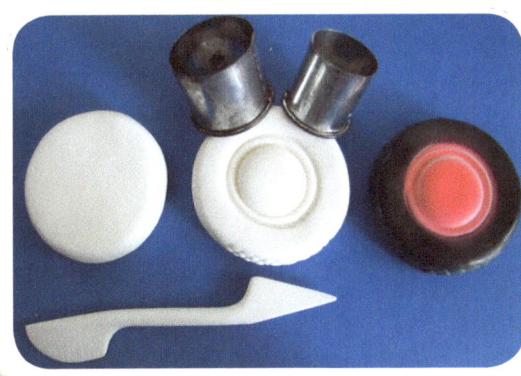

Rock Sugar

Used for rocks, snow scenes, coral and fizzy from a bottle.

STAGES	INGREDIENTS	WEIGHT	%
A	Sugar	500	**100**
	Water	125	**25**
B	Well beaten royal icing	1 teaspoon	
	Totals	**625**	**125**

Rock sugar is an old decorating item once used extensively on Christmas cakes as snow. It has a honeycomb interior and can be coloured by adding coloured royal icing or by spraying with an air brush.

It is made by boiling "A" to hard crack (160C) stirring until the mixture boils and then, from time to time, washing the pan down with water using a pastry brush to prevent crystals forming on the sides of the pan. Once the sugar starts to boil stop stirring.

Add "B" (the well beaten royal icing)

Whisk the royal icing into the boiling sugar, the mixture will rise in the saucepan because of the tiny air bubbles expanding through the heat.

Once the mixture subsides it is immediately poured into a container (I used an eight inch cake pan) lined with aluminium foil which has been sprayed with oil, prepare this before you start).

The mixture will rise again to the top of the cake pan and as it cools and sets. It will drop back slightly.

Allow it cool completely after which it can be sawn into pieces or broken up.

Other uses can be for scenery, lunar-scapes, coral, the texture of bread crumb and bubbly coming out of a champagne bottle. The pieces can be sprayed with colour to add depth or the colour can be added in with the royal icing at the boiling stage or added during the boiling process.

Isomalt

Used for ponds and the tears and pool of water of the crocodile.

STAGES	INGREDIENTS	WEIGHT	%
A	Isomalt	300	**100**
	Water	100	**33**
	Totals	**400**	**133**

Place the isomalt and water into a clean saucepan (copper or stainless steel.

Boil to 165°C, no acid or glucose/corn syrup is needed.

Pull as for pulled sugar. For cast pieces it has better fluidity than boiled sugar which allows it to run into small areas better.

For the crocodile tears the isomalt is very carefully poured into a silicone paper piping bag – only half fill the bag as it may come out of the top while piping.

Due to the extreme heat of the liquid isomalt I recommend that you wear gloves when piping isomalt, I also wrap the paper cone in a tea towel.

Display pieces made from isomalt tend not to crystallize or go sticky so quickly. High humidity tends to only cause a loss of gloss without dissolving occurring. Boiled isomalt has a purer white colour and does take on a yellow tinge like boiled sugar does. It can also be worked at lower temperatures than boiled sugar can which provides for a longer working time. Isomalt also has the added advantage that it can be reheated several times without crystallization occurring.

Its main draw-back is the cost so if you can't afford to use isomalt or it is too difficult to obtain in your area use ordinary sugar.

About the Author

MICHAEL GODDARD decorated his first cake way back when he was 16 years old and since then he has been in great demand for the quality of his work.

He first trained as a chef, after that he travelled to the Dorchester Hotel in London and then on to work at the Bellevue Palace Hotel, Berne, Switzerland where he started to learn sugar work in the patisserie section under Willy Graff, the then pastry chef of the Swiss national culinary team.

On returning to the UK, Mike went back to the College of Food in Birmingham to graduate in Advanced Bread Making, Advanced Flour Confectionery (Pastry Cooking), Design and Decoration of Flour Confectionery (Cake Decoration) and Advanced Certificate Hotel Patisserie (dist). It was here, in 1975, that he met George Stevens (see front of book) who encouraged him in the art of cake decorating and especially marzipan modelling. It was between his first and second year that Mike worked as a cake decorator at one of Birmingham's premier cake decorating departments helping to supply 30 shops.

Mike was chef patissier at the Albany Hotel Birmingham, where he was seconded to the Cumberland Hotel in London for the Queen's garden parties at Buckingham Palace.

After a further two years as a pastry chef lecturer in a small college, where he worked alongside George Stevens, Mike returned to the Birmingham College of Food in the bakery section as a lecturer where he taught cake decoration and other aspects of baking for more than eight years. It was at this time Mike was requested to make numerous cakes for various civic occasions and charities.

Meanwhile Mike met his future wife Trudie, also a qualified baker, pastry-cook and cake decorator, and after their wedding and honeymoon they opened a cake decorating shop in Walsall from which they supplied over twenty shops with celebration cakes.

A new chapter started for Mike and Trudie's young family when they immigrated to Australia in 1990. Mike was employed by Swan TAFE in WA and after winning the National Australian Baking Scholarship was offered a position at CIT (TAFE) in Canberra where he became Acting Head of Baking, Butchery and Advanced Cookery. At this time the wind changed again and off he went to Tasmania where he has now made his home. Working at Drysdale Institute in Hobart, Mike has been teaching baking and patisserie students his favourite subjects – cake decorating and sugar modelling.

Committed to not only teach but to further his skills, Mike also has two diplomas from Ewald Notter's Sugar school when based in Switzerland and has trained at Savour patisserie and chocolate school in Melbourne.

In addition, Mike has been a regular contributor in magazines across Australia writing for "The Australian Pastrycooks' and Bakers'", "Bakers' News", "The Leading Edge" and "Australian Sugar Craft".

Always in demand, Mike has been a judge and Chief Judge for various Baking competitions and Salon Culinaires both in and out of Tasmania.

In 2011, Mike decided he would start another cake decorating business and opened "Angel Cakes" near Hobart where he creates bespoke cakes. In its first year of business Angel Cakes was awarded

- 2012 Tasmanian Baking Awards – One Gold, one silver and Champion entry for cakes and pastries categories
- 2012 Wrest Point Fine Foods Awards – Three Gold, one silver, one bronze and Reserve Grand Champion for cakes and pastries categories.

The latest addition to his business is a teaching facility where he offers classes on various subjects of cake decorating and baking.

This is Mike's first book and he hopes you add it to your library and find it a great help making our Wild and Whacky Australian animals. Although designed for cake decorating the models can also be made from clay and plasticine.

Happy Modelling

Photo by Luke Goddard

Mike's newest venture is a new cake artistry studio based in Tasmania which will not only make and decorate cakes but will also offer lessons to small groups and one on one for cake decorating, chocolate and modelling.

He is also accepting invitations for demonstration requests and workshops both in Australia and worldwide.

For further information contact Mike on angelcakes1951@yahoo.com.au

First published in Australia 2013

Text copyright © 2013 in Michael Goddard
Photo copyright © 2013 in Michael Goddard
Photo copyright © 2013 page 99 in Luke Goddard
Design layout © 2013 in Sandra Dillon

The moral right of the author has been asserted.

All rights reserved. No part of this book may be used or reproduced in any manner whatsoever without written permission from the publisher except in the case of brief quotations used in critical articles or review.

Published by Bake Train
3 Coach Road, Chigwell, Tasmania, Australia 7011
Phone: 0477 874019
Email: baketrain@gmx.com
Find Bake Train on Facebook

A CIP catalogue record for this book is available from the National Library of Australia.

ISBN 13: 978 0 9875939 0 0

2 0 1 3 1 2 3 4 5 6 7 8

Text by Michael Goddard
Photography by Michael Goddard *(page 99 by Luke Goddard)*
Models created and made by Michael Goddard
Design layout and artwork by Sandra Dillon